Making Movies Without Losing Money

This book is about the practical realities of the film market today and how to make a film while minimizing financial risk. Film is a risky investment and securing that investment is a huge challenge. The best way to get investors is to do everything possible to make the film without losing money.

Featuring interviews with film industry veterans – sales agents, producers, distributors, directors, film investors, film authors and accountants – Daniel Harlow explores some of the biggest obstacles to making a commercially successful film and offers best practice advice on making a good film that will also be a commercial success. The book explores key topics such as smart financing, casting to add value, understanding the film supply chain, the importance of genre, picking the right producer, negotiating presales and much more. By learning how to break even, this book provides invaluable insight into the film industry that will help filmmakers build a real, continuing career.

A vital resource for filmmakers serious about sustaining a career in the 21st-century film industry.

Daniel Harlow, a Departmental Scholar from UCLA, founded a technology consulting firm in 1993 which grew to 300 employees in six offices around the country. After selling his company, Harlow attended the Independent Film Producer Program at UCLA. He is currently the founder and CEO of a new hi-tech startup, Bunker 15 Films, with the mission to help indie films find their audience through Smart Publicity and Promotional programs. Harlow believes that with good technology and good planning filmmakers can sustain financially rewarding careers.

Making Movies Without Losing Money

Practical Lessons in Film Finance

Daniel Harlow

Routledge
Taylor & Francis Group

LONDON AND NEW YORK

First published 2020
by Routledge
2 Park Square, Milton Park, Abingdon, Oxon OX14 4RN

and by Routledge
52 Vanderbilt Avenue, New York, NY 10017

Routledge is an imprint of the Taylor & Francis Group, an informa business

© 2020 Daniel Harlow

British Library Cataloguing-in-Publication Data
A catalogue record for this book is available from the British Library

Library of Congress Cataloging-in-Publication Data
Names: Harlow, Daniel, author.
Title: Making movies without losing money:
practical lessons in film finance / Daniel Harlow.
Description: London; New York: Routledge, 2020. |
Includes index. Identifiers: LCCN 2019055882 (print) |
LCCN 2019055883 (ebook) | ISBN 9780367369781 (hardback) |
ISBN 9780429352157 (ebook)
Subjects: LCSH: Motion pictures–Production and direction. |
Motion picture industry–Finance.
Classification: LCC PN1995.9.P7 H358 2020 (print) |
LCC PN1995.9.P7 (ebook) | DDC 791.4302/32–dc23
LC record available at https://lccn.loc.gov/2019055882
LC ebook record available at https://lccn.loc.gov/2019055883

ISBN: 978-0-367-36978-1 (hbk)
ISBN: 978-0-429-35215-7 (ebk)

Typeset in Times New Roman
by Newgen Publishing UK

Contents

Introduction

A film is, without doubt, a work of art. But unlike a novelist, or a painter, who can work alone, a film is a massive undertaking requiring a sizeable team and high-tech equipment. It could be one person's vision, but it requires the participation of many artists. You could be that one person with a vision. In fact, you could be the Jimi Hendrix of film-making, the cinematic version of Beethoven. You could be the most gifted writer/director/producer in history were it not for the biggest obstacle to today's filmmaker: money.

Would the world ever know Mozart's Magic Flute if he had to raise $1M in funding before he could play a note? Would we ever have seen Picasso's Blue Period if he had to spend a year convincing investors of his vision before he could pick up a paintbrush?

This book traces my journey from tech entrepreneur to the industry of film – specifically, investment and production. After I sold my IT company of 20 years, I set up a film fund. I began negotiations to produce a slate of three low-budget indie movies. But I was stopped cold when no one could tell me how these movies would make their money back. *Whoa*, I thought, *hold the phone! That's a big blind spot.*

The realization inspired what turned out to be a multi-year tangent where I spent most of my time interviewing industry professionals about the financial fate of films. Often the conversation was about why small films lose money and what smart people are doing to make sure it doesn't happen to them.

If you're a filmmaking hopeful having trouble raising funds, it's probably because of one very good reason: without a clear plan for how your film will make money, you're almost certain to lose money. No gimmicky fund-raising tip is going to change that fact. Investors are steering away from you, not because they are stupid, but because they are smart. People with money (as a rule) don't want to lose it.

It turns out that filmmakers who find "new money" (investors that have never invested in film before) – then lose it – have a hard time sustaining a career. They're basically starting from zero with their next movie, having burned all their investors with their first. Meanwhile, real career film professionals work with "smart money" (investors that routinely invest in film) and make sure to make the money back.

The advice those professionals would give to first-time filmmakers is what makes up this book. Making art for a living has never been easy and the new dynamics of the film world – streaming, piracy, video-on-demand (VOD), etc. – has made it even trickier. But if you are willing to put a business hat on top of your creative hat, then it can be done.

Filmmaking is now theoretically possible with just an iPhone, a computer for editing and no money. No-budget filmmaking or guerilla filmmaking is possible but in practice, no-budget filmmaking is limited to weekend film shoots with friends – i.e. making short films for fun. As anyone that has made a serious attempt of making a film will tell you, this sport still costs real money.

You can't get a crew to work for free for a 2–3 week film shoot. Elaborate sound equipment is still required. Legal work is necessary if you want your film to be publicly available. Even if you work with a skeleton team – as suggested by Ed Burns in his famous indie filmmaker manual *Independent Ed* – you still have five to six people to pay. And that's with no lighting equipment, hoping mother nature is on your side so you can film with natural light. Post-production is still required. Professional (paid) actors are highly recommended if you want to end up with a watchable product. The Screen Actors Guild (SAG) contracts specify ultra-low budget films have budgets under $250K but calling it "ultra-low" doesn't make it easy to get a quarter of a million dollars from an investor.

When it comes to the relationship between funding, filmmakers and actually making real movies, I learned one important lesson when I attended Austin's renowned film conference, South by Southwest (SXSW): filmmakers spend a lot of time begging for money. In early March, when SXSW fills the streets of Austin with people wearing "Filmmaker" badges, the Intercontinental Hotel downtown is flooded with filmmakers and they all – well, nine out of ten of them anyway – are looking for funding for a film.

If you want funding for your film, you could beg, borrow, network, schmooze and cold-call. But even if you do get lucky, you might end up like a growing number of one-time filmmakers that – having lost six figures of someone else's money – now can't get funding for their second film. First-time filmmakers often have this misguided impression that all they need is that ONE break. If they can just make that ONE movie, then the world will recognize them for their talents, but that's not how it works. Having lost the investment on one film, you are not in a better position to get funding for your second – you're in a worse position.

Two years ago, I set out with a theory. And that theory stands up well today: the best way to get film investors interested is to have a good film investment in the first place, and; the best way to get investors interested a second time is to make money for your first investors.

If you're interested in this approach, then this is the book you want to read.

You will also want to read this book because set before you is opportunity like the film industry has never seen before. There is unprecedented demand for video content. Netflix, Hulu, HBO, YouTube Red, Amazon Prime and Apple TV are just the top tier of literally hundreds of streaming services to which customers can subscribe. Each streaming service, and every cable TV station and network, is vying to attract viewers with original content. Each of these video delivery channels is making their own original content. They need, as it happens, filmmakers! If you can make films without losing money, you'll be in high-demand. But how to start?

The best way to secure funding for your first feature is by having a plan to make back your investor's money, plus a profit. The best way to secure a career in film is by making sure those plans work over and over again. This book aims to bridge the gap between the filmmakers who desperately want to make film and the demand for the content. This book is for that currently unknown Mozart or Picasso of filmmaking out there that is spending all their time begging for funding, trying to find a high-wealth individual that will take a chance on them, trying to build a career taking shortcuts. Investors are getting too smart and money is now too tight. Investors are looking for films that will pay off and not just be glamourous.

Mozart made a comfortable living as a musician. Picasso died with a fortune of over $100M.

Even if you're a genius, the best way to create and sustain a career in art is by making movies that make money.

Part 1
One small problem

1 A surprising discovery

Independent filmmakers have a problem: they lose money. And I don't mean marginally or some small percentage of their film's investment. Often the investment is completely lost. All of it. This would appear to be an ever-so-small problem to most laypeople.

My education is not in film. I'm coming at this from an outside point of view. I ran a successful IT consulting firm for 20 years, sold it, retired and played golf for a year – long enough to know that a year is more than enough golf for a lifetime. Ready to come out of retirement, I wanted to try my hand at being a movie producer. I started a film fund and began interviewing filmmakers to make a film. Things started to go south quickly once I asked the filmmakers: "So how do we monetize the film once it's done? How does the film make back the money?" Once I asked that question, I got a mix of annoyance, silence or just general gurgling. I quickly realized that I needed to figure this out since no one else seemed to know.

From one point of view, you might say my background is pretty good for filmmaking. I built my company with no outside funding from one employee to 300. From zero offices to six. Similar to indie filmmakers, I regularly competed with teams that had substantially more people and money than I did. Not a little more money but a factor of 100 or 1,000 times more capital. And not a few more employees than my firm but they would be staffed at a level ten times larger than mine. And yet I won business and captured market share repeatedly, beating large competition in almost every competitive situation. I captured the attention of customers and got them to buy with creativity. I knew my customers, my audience, better. I used my limited resources to create an experience that stood out from the crowd even while others were better funded and better staffed. In short, we made magic happen with pennies and with very few people – people that were young, inexperienced, but motivated. I thought I could make the same magic happen in the entertainment industry, so off I went.

I wanted to make movies, yes, but I didn't want to throw money away. There are lots of charities to give money to. If I was going to knowingly toss money away, I can think of many worthy causes. And even if it wasn't my money, I didn't want to lose other people's money either.

Plus, I didn't want to just make one movie. I wanted to build a career in film which is hard, I would imagine, to do by making films that don't recoup their investment. A sustainable career in really any field is based on breaking even or making a profit.

Knowing how hard it might be to make a good movie without losing the investor's money, I went about learning all there was to know about movies and money. After all, I didn't want a movie all finished and done and then find out I did it the wrong way or I should have done something at the very beginning of the process that I didn't learn until it was too late! I spent two years learning everything there was to know about movies and money.

What does the industry say about indies and money?

What do you learn about making a financially successful film when you spend $1K+ to attend SXSW in Austin, filling your days with one-on-one mentor sessions, round table discussions and inspirational keynotes? In Chapter 2, I cover one of the most repeated lessons on "Looking for answers at festivals."

What do you learn about making film without losing money when you attend UCLA's Certificate program for Independent Film Producing – staffed by the best and the brightest from the professional ranks of working film industry personnel? It is covered later in this Part.

Or when you spend countless hours online watching filmmaker speeches by Mark Duplass, Ava DuVernay and others – or read Ed Burns, Robert Rodriguez' advice on making indie film on a budget?

We will discuss all of the above in the upcoming pages. I did all of this and then I set out on my own, with the guidance of the UCLA film studies faculty to interview 100+ working industry professionals to learn how to reliably make a financially successful film on a budget of less than $1M (the lower the better). My research steers clear from the "no-budget" films with less than $50K budgets because we are trying to find films that cost some money, which is the only way to figure out if they recouped an investment.

What made my research unique is that I did not sit down with only the creative contributors and filmmakers like writers, directors and production specialists. I focused on film *business* people. Sales agents, distribution experts, film accountants, film financiers, film lawyers, producers, and what I accumulated was – it seems to me – the largest research project to date about what makes an indie film financially successful.

I learned that the goal – to make money (or at least to not lose money) on a small budget film – was, well, very hard, to put it mildly. Pessimism is a mild word for the feeling I was confronted with. Making a financially profitable film for under a million dollars is a task with a failure rate that most estimated as well over 90%.

The problem with much of this pessimism is that it takes for granted a questionable assumption: that a filmmaker is only interested in making "their film, their way." The assumption implies that filmmakers are stubborn and uncompromising when it comes to their "artistic vision," and just not interested in making money. But after talking to a lot of them? My conclusion is: "Not so much."

Sure, some are this way. As much as the filmmaking "creatives" (as they are called) seem out of touch with the business people, the reverse is often equally true. Filmmakers want to make a film – hopefully a good film. But let's be honest: a bad film that people watch is, by far, preferable to not making any film at all. In fact, there are a lot of benefits (that are not lost on filmmakers) to making a commercially successful film even if it's not in Oscar contention the year it comes out. So the pessimism is warranted IF you're making a "personal film" with an "uncompromising artistic vision" and you have no plan for how you're going to sell it once it's done. If you are making a film that's good, and you make it with a plan, then your odds of making the investment back are going to skyrocket. If your plan starts even before you have a script, then your odds go up further. Commercially viable films are as hard to make as critically acclaimed films. They involve all aspects of the filmmaking process from casting, producing, writing, budgeting and picking the right genre. They are meticulously planned in partnership with people that have experience. They don't come together on a Red-Bull-fueled weekend of inspiration.

How the book is organized: common themes and unconventional advice

The book presents the obstacles first for good reason. Throughout my research, the same types of obstacles came up again and again. They fall into different categories but they repeatedly came up. The obstacles – and the keys to getting around them – should be well understood by an aspiring filmmaker. As you might expect, I discovered the obstacles first. When the Wright Brothers created their flying machine, they hit the ground many times before it flew. The solutions come after becoming very familiar with the problems. Thus, I lay out the varying issues and challenges of the film industry as I encountered them. Then I present some ideas for solutions.

I offer a detailed discussion on the business of film. What happens to a film after it is finished? This discussion is important when you think about monetizing the film and recouping the budget in order to break even or make a profit. Understanding the logistics of the film business is as important to making a successful film career as knowing the rules of football if you want to play football and win games. A director or writer who wants their picture to be a financial success without knowing the business side of film is like an actor who can't be bothered to promote their own films. Acting in the film isn't the only job. Promoting the film is key. For a filmmaker, it isn't just making a good film. Knowing the bottom line matters to the people that funded the project.

Then I go over to the best practices suggested to me again and again when you want to make a film that makes its budget back. The practices run the gamut from development, production, financing, etc., almost every aspect of the filmmaking process is addressed.

I know that you might be tempted to skip straight to the solutions. However I urge you to bear with me and wallow in the challenges and problems before jumping straight there.

Primarily, this recommendation is because knowing the problem well is always more important than memorizing a pre-packaged solution. Understanding the challenges is like looking at a map of the territory. Look at a map of California and you can instinctively understand the difficulties in getting from San Francisco to Napa Valley, considering the bays, the ocean and the river. I can give you a detailed description of multiple different routes from San Francisco to Napa Valley but if you know the territory, you might be able to find your own way. You may even decide to use a hot air balloon so all that water in between might not concern you as much anymore. If you understand the issues thoroughly, you can improvise your own solutions, come up with your own formulas that fit your goals and might be significantly more creative and successful than the ones I present here.

What this book is not

This is not a book about how to make your movie, your way. The desire to make a "personal movie" with total freedom was expressed so often from the creative side of the filmmaking industry that it became some-what of a common refrain: "I want to make my movie, my way" the phrase would go. If you want to make your movie your way then you should (and I'm being serious) use *your* money.

This is not a book about how to make a giant, great big, massive HIT. If this book were about making a hit, it would be far easier to write and research. Box office returns are the only financials that are public and thus easily accessible. Researching what makes a hit would simply be a process of pulling out the box office financials of the top 100 indies, finding commonalities and publishing the results. This book isn't about how a small number of big winners managed to get lucky and strike it rich. It is about how the every-day, blue-collar producers place their bets strategically to tilt the odds in their favor and minimize the chances they will walk away from a project as a loser, financially

Lastly, this is not a book about how to make the actual movie. There are many books like this already. Guerilla filmmaking, low budget film-making, indie producing, etc., are all topics that are well covered by books that are already out there. Authors like Suzanne Lyons have covered them well. For the most part, those books stop upon comple-tion of the film.

I had initially thought this book would pick up where those books left off. It would discuss what to do once the film was done. But in fact, the process of building a commercially successful film starts much earlier. But I'm getting ahead of myself.

I had better take the advice of the king in Alice in Wonderland and simply begin at the beginning.

2 The journey begins

During my efforts to make a film, it became apparent that a lot of film makers don't understand the financial end of the industry. In particular, many don't know how a film drives revenues and recoups the initial investment. There are a myriad of reasons for this (that I'll get into later). I sat down and began a quest to find people who did know and who would share the information. It wasn't as easy as I had thought it would be. When I did speak with people knowledgeable on the subject, they weren't optimistic about the chances of small films being profitable.

To imagine what it's like to search for a reliable and profitable business model in film, I think it best to imagine yourself in the opening sequence of Francis Ford Coppola's *Apocalypse Now*. Helicopters flying over, explosions, destruction and fire. Roughly a third of my conversations with film industry veterans were of this nature: "This industry is a burning building and you'd be crazy to run inside."

It's hard to imagine an industry as ubiquitous, international and glamourous as film being "in trouble" but the changes in the industry have caused many businesses to fold. Only the smartest will survive. Education and positioning are key.

Turmoil was a word that kept popping up. As in: "The film industry is in turmoil." Huge sources of revenue have dried up from DVD sales and theatrical ticket sales. These revenues have not been replaced (at least not yet) from the digital analogy of DVD sales, pay-per-view TVOD (Transactional Video-On-Demand) sales from such platforms as Amazon or iTunes.

On the flip side, the cost of making a film has dropped, and as a result the market is flooded with product. There are many new channels that are creating a lot of original content (which creates fantastic opportunity for filmmakers) but these buyers are hesitant to buy independent films from new filmmakers. They are making their own films or buying from reliable sources where they get consistently the types of films they expect. It all adds up to them being less inclined than ever to buy your film. The downward trend in demand and the upward trend in supply of new indies throws more turmoil into the industry.

If the story prologue is helicopters and explosions, then this would be the opening credits:

> This is a true story. The events and the conversations depicted in this book are real. The names have been changed to protect the innocent (or the guilty, depending on how you look at it). I have conducted 100+ interviews from film professionals – film sales executives, distributors, producers, film financiers or accountants, and development professionals. The conversations were candid and nearly everyone requested their comments be "off-the-record."

In *Apocalypse Now*, this would be the scene where Martin Sheen blinks and sees he's still only in Saigon. But instead, he'd look outside and see he's in Austin, Texas and it's 2018. "What am I doing here?" Martin would ask. The answer: trying to find a way to make a film and not lose money.

Act one – looking for the answer at film festivals

It was around $1K to buy my film conference ticket at SXSW (cheaper if you pay well in advance, which I didn't). What did I learn? One lesson I learned was the same from Blake Synder's *Save the Cat*: what's really important is the film's title and logline.

> Title: To make an indie
> Logline: One filmmaker, against the odds, forges ahead while an industry toils. A thriller with an ending that no one can (ever) predict.
> Fade in – SXSW 2018 – a roundtable discussion

Frank and I sit at the round table discussion. He's an Austin filmmaker with a big burly beard, slicked-back ponytail and a burning gaze. Frank punctuates his sentences with a verbal exclamation point that tells you that if he says he's going to do something, you can rest assured, it'll get done. Frank is hardcore. He pays the rent by shooting rock music videos and if he showed up to shoot your rock music video, you'd think: "Yep, that's how a guy that films rock music videos should look." Frank wants to make a movie – badly. He's filmed his own short. He's filmed his own reel. He'll hand you a jump drive with it on there. It's not half bad. And he's shelled out the $1K for the filmmaker pass at SXSW to hear what the experts have to say.

We look up to these filmmakers that are showing a film at SXSW. And we should. Austin's SXSW is known as one of the top festivals and top film conferences in the US. If it's anything like Sundance (who makes their number of submissions public) they have had an exploding number of submissions. Sundance had only 250 submissions in 1993 (giving you over a 50% chance of being accepted). Isn't that depressing? Because now, over 14,000 films, shorts and episodics are submitted yearly to Sundance and only about 1.5% of those projects get shown at the festival.

We think: "How do WE get to where THEY are, with a film in SXSW?" Tell us. Teach us. Frank and I spent hours and hours over the last three days talking to industry experts in one-on-one sessions, round tables discussions and listening to panels. What do they say?

One of the more sought-after experts at SXSW is a manager associated with a recent Oscar winner. His advice is clear: "Do work," he says. "Make something." Yeah, make something. Stop screwing around and yacking and being a pretender. Make a movie. I feel ya on that. You ask ten people at SXSW what they are doing and nine of them will say: "I'm working on a film." After a little while, once this answer starts to feel a bit, well, stale, I learn to ask the follow-up: "What stage are you in?" Expecting to hear: pre-production, post-production, filming starts next month, promoting, whatever. But I don't hear that even once. The answer you get in almost every case is: "I'm looking for funding." As an entrepreneur that ran a business for a couple decades, it's hard for me not to kink my neck at that answer. Ok. *So if you're looking for funding, you're NOT really working on a film.* I get Mr. Oscar-Winner-Manager's advice: "Stop looking for funding. Do something."

Ava DuVernay (*Selma, A Girl's Trip, A Wrinkle in Time*) has a 2013 Film Independent keynote address on YouTube with thousands of views where she speaks about the number of people that ask to sit down with her and "pick her brain." She pounds her podium and tells people that want mentoring and advice to "knock it off."

> All that energy, all that focus on trying to extract from other people is preventing you from doing … the only thing that moves you forward is your work.
>
> (Ava Duvernay, 2013, Keynote Address, Film Independent Forum)

Mark Duplass has a well-received YouTube video where he spoke, coincidentally, at SXSW. His advice: first, make a short film. Then take $1K, buy food, pay for all the equipment you need with credit cards at Best Buy and Home Depot and return it all when you're done. Make a film. With a voice. Stop sitting around and thinking about it.

Frank and I are now sipping our two free drinks at the bar at the Intercontinental Hotel at SXSW. It's best to get both free drinks at the same time, therefore avoiding the lengthy bar line the second time #WeRPros #DoubleFisting. We are catching more experts in between beers, asking more advice. We tell them about the films we'd like to make and our plans to market them. One after the other, they give some version of: "Finish your movie, then get back to me."

The experts have spoken and the ruling is unanimous. Make a film. First. Make it good and worry about the rest once it's finished. If you build it, they will come.

Listen, I get it. Ava, Mark, Mr. Oscar winner, they all talk to people all day long that will never, ever, in a million years, make a movie. I get their frustration and I hear their message. So should you. But I can't help feeling there is something dismissive in their advice. It might not be flat out wrong but it seems unnecessarily extreme to tell people to go from analysis-paralysis to suddenly go to a strategy of: fire first, aim second. I ran a successful company for a long time and that doesn't fit my personal investment style, nor my management style – nor my anything style actually.

And, do studios make films this way? Um, no. Do I want to put up $100K of my own money into a film without the foggiest notion of what will happen once it's done? Um, no. But I need to give these experts the benefit of the doubt. So I resolve to go find some filmmakers that followed this advice and see how it went. SXSW closes. FADE OUT.

Act two – tracking down those who "just did it"

FADE IN – later that year – Cucalorus Film Festival, Wilmington, NC.

Katherine has made a solid independent film. She sits across from me with her new daughter in a lovely coffee shop unusually crowded due to the influx of visitors from the festival. We are lucky to get the two couches with the coffee table in between giving her and her daughter extra room. Katherine raised around $300K to make her personal film that has received strong reviews for its sensitive drama and sense of humor from multiple, small festivals. I discuss with her how she feels it will do financially and she deadpans: "I doubt it will make much, if anything, really and I'm not concerned about that. I just want to get it on Netflix, even if we need to take little or no money for it, since that exposure is really important for my future projects." Little or no money?

"How much do you expect to recoup from the $300K investment?" I asked. "Probably nothing or almost nothing" was her answer. From a $300K investment to recoup $0? "Almost zero," she says. Oh.

FADE IN – later that day – different coffee shop

Peter sits across from me wondering how in the world his tiny film with just two actors managed to cost $250K. He was the director and not the producer so he wasn't sure what cost so much but he knows that was his budget. His film won distribution by a very large, well-known distribution firm. They, of course, will pay him nothing up front for the film. Zero. But he'll make a percentage, right? Yes, he says. After they recoup their costs. What costs, I ask? He has no idea – but whatever they are doing, it will cost him some $30K of his film's first revenues. He believes all they are doing is putting it on iTunes, which costs about $1,200. But they did sell the film to Hulu for $35K – almost all of which the distribution company will keep. His investors will make a few thousand dollars back. Out of a $250K investment? Yes, he says. And he knows many of his peers are in the same situation.

"We can never use the same investors twice. It's just a process of burning through investors," says Peter. Okay then. "There must be a better way," I say. He agrees. Absolutely. He just doesn't know how. He has no clue how to make a profitable film. "I'd make a zombie movie if you told me it would make money. I'd make a movie about two stoner skateboarder kids fighting zombies if you told me that would make money." What makes money?

Indeed. What makes money?

If this were *Apocalypse Now*, we'd be at the scene when Martin Sheen sits with G.D. Spradlin and Harrison Ford and they give him his mission. Find Kurtz. I've been given a mission: What makes money? Everyone gets everything they want. I wanted a mission. And for my sins, they gave me one.

Act three – and for my sins, they gave me one

I began to suspect that not all my answers could be discovered over two free beers at the Intercontinental in Austin or in coffee shops in Wilmington, NC. I began to seek out other, denser sources – preferably from actual practitioners that were as concerned about the financial sustainability of a film career as they were about the critical acceptance of the films.

As luck would have it, I'm a UCLA alumni – and I say lucky because UCLA has one of the very few post-grad academic programs for the study of film. And they have a fantastic one at that. Not exclusively the craft of film, but the business of film is taught there. The school, the courses, the material are amazing. The execution of online course work is outstanding. The faculty and staff are, across the board, superstars. If you want to learn about film, this is the place. That said, the message relayed in the courses seems to be the same message found in the majority of film books currently for sale: the GOAL is the finished film. Getting the film done is the primary, secondary and final objective. There are some cursory words perhaps on marketing to demographics on social media or on how to approach festivals but not much stated about how to make sure the film investment is returned or secured. The objective it seems has always been the making of a film – not the making of money from a film.

They offered a Certificate Program in Independent Film Producing. Exactly what I was looking for. I enrolled and took business film classes but most of them still fell short of tackling the challenge of film profitability. The class on low-budget filmmaking, again, focused exclusively on getting the film made and not what to do with it when it's done. There's discussion of budgets but nothing much on how to secure those funds and nothing on how to recoup them. There was a course on indie film marketing and distribution which I assumed was my Holy Grail. Surely this course – the only one apparently about what to do with a film after it's done, would have to discuss monetizing the film. But alas most of the examples in the film marketing class assumed a marketing budget of at least six to seven figures (i.e. just the marketing budget, not the total film's budget). Now this is a reasonable assumption, knowing that most of your class would go on to work in the marketing departments of large Los Angeles-based studios. But if you're looking to make a low budget film where your marketing budget is far less than $100K then the information was less useful.

However, there was a small footnote to students about applying for your own self-determined "independent study" course where you set the agenda yourself. Fantastic. I created my own independent study and got approval from UCLA to spend the entire time researching how to make an indie film profitably – budgets between $100K and $1M.

With the course approval in hand, interviewing real life current film practitioners would be the core of the research – along with analyzing as much data as I could gather – which wasn't much. More on that later.

I decided to shoot for the moon. On my list to interview was Roger Corman, king of the B-movie. Roger Corman started his career in the 1950s with films like *Attack of the Crab Monsters* (1957) and *Little Shop of Horrors* (1960). His wild, low-budget films fueled an empire that continued with *Death Race 2000* (1975) and *Slumber Party Massacre* (1982). It turned out, this film career was not to be a flash-in-the-pan. The audience still watches *Death Race 2500* (2017) and *Slumber Party Massacre 3* (1990). He literally wrote a book called *How I Made a Hundred Movies in Hollywood and Never Lost a Dime*.

John Sloss was also on top of my list because of his work with Ed Burns, during which Burns wrote *Independent Ed*. John seemed to be pioneering in the areas of new-paradigm film production and distribution. Certainly he would have insight into how these new methods and technologies were affecting film financials. I was interested to talk to Burns and his colleagues. My biggest concern was that since he wrote *Independent Ed*, which had some impressive case studies in the methods of profitable low-budget indie filmmaking, he had mostly stopped his low-budget filmmaking. This was a troublesome sign that perhaps he found a way to do it but, in the end, it was too much trouble, too little reward. I never did get my answer from Burns on why he stopped making indies. Life gets busy sometimes. Let's hope we hear more from Ed in the upcoming years. Until then I have a whole long list of people to talk to.

I begin with my list, starting at the top.

I emailed the guru of B-Movies, Roger Corman. Within hours, he emailed back! Wow. But oh, it's not him. It's his assistant. I spoke with one of his development professionals. Not a bad start, though. I emailed John Sloss. And HE emailed back – wait – again, it's his assistant but I talk to someone at his firm. A lot of people have a lot to say on this subject. I had hit a nerve, struck the proverbial chord, hit the vein of oil – people were in the mood to talk about this – I had dug and found a goldmine of information. It was easier to get information from real professionals than I had thought possible. My goal was 10–12 professional interviews and when I was done, I had over 100!

But how will the "just do it" advice – that I had heard from SXSW speakers, DuVernay, Duplass and the like – jive with what these professionals know about finance and film? I know that the "just do it" advice didn't appear to reap large financial rewards for the handful of filmmakers that I interviewed that had actually gone out and "done it," but perhaps the sample size of my interviews was too small. Perhaps if I broadened my view, I would find people who had better luck with the "build it and they will come" strategy.

I told many of the industry people I was interviewing the SXSW stories. I asked them about the "just do it" advice given out at film conferences. I figured they would largely agree but qualify their answers in some way. I expected to hear: "Yes, absolutely. Go out and make a small, cheap film then ... (fill in the blank)." I just didn't know what would end up filling in the blank.

"What do you think about the predominant advice to filmmakers of 'just do it' or 'go make work'?" I asked.

"The dumbest advice I've ever heard," said one sales executive. Hardly the due respect normally given to Oscar winners! Maybe that was a fluke. I'll ask another guy: "Possibly, the stupidest thing that you could tell a filmmaker," said another. Oh boy, two for two disrespecting the experts at film festivals! Maybe it was a sales agent thing. I'll talk to a distributor next.

The distributor, having gotten the gist of my question, couldn't contain his frustration. He cuts me off before I can finish. He wanted to ask me something – off-the-record of course.

"Why do filmmakers make these movies – for these festivals – that no one wants to see? Why do they make this crap?" He even goes so far to ask me to go online and look up a film (a "festival film") that's packed with stars. It had so many famous people, I might want to see it. I asked, "When is that coming out?" He almost shouted through the phone, "That came out nine months ago!" he said. "But you don't know, right? Because it tanked. The movie was a snore. I distributed that piece of shit and it's made nothing. With all that star power and they make THAT movie? Why? If I had those actors with a $750K budget, I could make a $30M profit!"

Strictly speaking, his theory that he could have made a more profitable movie with that same star power doesn't totally hold up. It's likely those actors made themselves available (at a lower salary) precisely because of the "thoughtful" (kind word) nature of that film. There's a good chance that what sold those actors on that project was precisely because it was not typical commercial fare. And it's therefore likely they would not have jumped at the chance to be in a more conventionally commercial film. However, his point is still strong. If you manage to get star power in your film, use it, don't throw it away on a snooze of a film. There is a line the smart filmmaker must walk: create a role that actors want to play so they are attracted to your material, but the film must ultimately be watchable and earn a wide audience.

Those actors will more likely be in your next movie (again at a lower salary) if your unconventional film manages to find a huge audience. Ask Quentin Tarantino about that.

Still another distributor warned of a depressing reality: "I know it's hard for many filmmakers to hear when they worked on a film for one or two years but many times their films are worthless, not worth very little – literally worth nothing, zero." And when he says zero – he means it. For many, many films, there are no buyers. Even if you give your film away for nothing, the buying distribution company must invest money to distribute it within their territory. Therefore, if they don't think your film will make a ripple in a pond, then they will end up wasting valuable time and money invested in its distribution. Therefore, he's right. For many films, no one wants them at all – even for free.

It seems people on the business side of film don't take kindly to the strategy of: "ready, fire, aim." And before they tell me about what they think filmmakers should do, they first vent – a lot – on what the industry as a whole, is up against. Their comments began to sound familiar. I was hearing the same problems again and again. I categorized them and listed them neatly for you below so you don't have to spend two years of your life like I did.

Let the venting begin.

Understanding the problem, at a deep level is always preferable to memorizing a formulaic solution.

Part 2
The obstacles

3 The culture of secrecy

Whether you know it or not, there's an elephant in the room or, better said, there's a gaping hole in this book. A blind spot so big that sometimes people don't even see it's there. Like asking fish what water is, it surrounds you and is such a part of your life, you don't even think about it anymore. What is the elephantine hole made of? Data. Clara Peller once stared down at a puny hamburger and said: "Where's the beef?" And likewise, an astute reader might flip through these pages and say: "Where's the data?"

I had anticipated half of my research would be dedicated to crunching data. When you run an IT company for 20 years, you are good at data analysis and you expect to do a lot of it. Comparing genre returns in foreign countries to domestic sales. Or comparing a comedy's performance in the US vs. the UK (does the sense of humor cross the ocean?). This part of the research is not going to happen, which is symptomatic of WHY filmmakers do have trouble making profitable films: i.e. no one has the information in this business. Those who do have it, won't share. And when they do share, the groups are so highly motivated to exaggerate, the numbers are not usable.

Whereas box office information is publicly available, this is not where most films make their money anymore. Box office data was useful in analyzing film industry trends decades ago but now foreign sales, online sales, VOD sales dominate small film revenues (while theatrical results are either non-existent, negligible, or a loss-lead – more on that later) and Amazon, Apple and Netflix are not going to hand over their data to anyone, let alone a researcher. If you want to research film performance in today's world, you must get proprietary information on private sales figures from agents and distributors. That's where you could get this information in bulk. And if you gathered enough of it, perhaps you could do a data analysis project worth something. However, this would mean gaining cooperation from a set of film industry companies that are not obligated nor motivated to share with you any data at all – and very unmotivated to share accurate data.

There are powerful motivations to hide or exaggerate financial performance data in film. Telling someone your real budget will mean either it's too low – thus your film will be pre-judged negatively for being "cheap" (so it can't be "good"). Or your budget is too high – in which case you've wasted your investors' money. It's a bit of a data catch-22: if your revenues are too low, you're a failure, but if your revenues are too high then everyone in the supply chain (sales agent, distributor, crew and talent) will have their hand out for their deferred payments or profit-sharing. If someone has the real numbers, what they tell you depends on their agenda and what they think you want to hear. No one ever hands over raw, accurate data.

The film business has a long history of secrecy. One of the film consultants I talked to explained it well:

> "You might be too young to remember," she said, "but the movie business – decades ago – was going to a theater and paying for ticket. It was a cash business. And what happens with cash businesses? A lot of that cash disappears at one point or another. It's impossible to audit. The mafia and other disreputable groups get involved. Everything was secret. The numbers you saw were never trustworthy and this veil of secrecy about who made how much (gross or profit) from where, it's still a big secret for the most part. It's impossible to get real numbers from anyone."

Depressingly, she was right. No agent nor distributor would give real financial results. The best I got was "we are in the black" or "we are not even close" or "we are close and probably in the next year we will be in the black." Filmmakers, agents, distributors and everyone else tend to be (slightly) more transparent about the *budgets* (as opposed to revenues) of the films, but there are obstacles there as well.

First, a distributor and a sales agent might not actually know the budget of a film. Similar to a real estate agent, it's not, strictly speaking, relevant. The only thing relevant is current market value. However, most filmmakers want to break even on a film. Therefore, most sales agents and distributors do know (could be exactly, could be roughly) the film's budget – since it constitutes an important target for success.

Second, filmmakers, producers, everyone are – once again – always giving you dodgy information. They don't want to give you the real budget, they want to double or triple it because films get pre-judged based on budget. No matter what the budget is, the filmmaker will hope you think it's 2–3 times that much. There is a stigma associated with films under $1M so all films want to appear to have at least $1M or else they will lack enough "production value" to be considered "good." On the other hand, they don't want to tell you the movie lost money either. Thus the complicated dance around the numbers. The movie is "in the black" – which is good. But if it is in the black because it was cheap to make – that is bad.

***

The data problem is real and it's a monster. Project Lodestar (www. projectlodestar.org) is a film project made up of volunteers that launched a website dedicated to the anonymous gathering of film industry data for indie films under $1M. It was designed to be a place where film industry personnel can send their *real* film financial results, anonymously, without being judged for being a failure. But there was no meaningful participation. The financial data gathering is still one of Lodestar's long-term goals but now they simply focus on how trends in film journalism impact indie filmmaking. More on that important dynamic later.

The lack of data handicaps those filmmakers most in need of the information. If filmmakers don't know what movies make money, then how are they supposed to make films that make money? If all filmmakers use a benchmark like *Little Miss Sunshine* and *Napoleon Dynamite* then they will think comedies rule. If they use *Paranormal Activity* and *The Blair Witch Project* as comparable films then found footage horror is the way to go. One sales agent was adamant at how risky comedies were, saying that humor doesn't travel internationally. And it doesn't even travel usually to the UK or Australia. The sense of humor can be very different in other (even English speaking) countries. If filmmakers saw real returns, actual sales figures for comedies that consistently showed a big drop-off from the US to the UK or Australia it might get a lot of filmmakers thinking hard about their next rom com.

Having good data on film results would be critical to indie filmmakers if it were available. This is yet another film dynamic that puts the little players at a disadvantage. Big studios stay ahead of the curve in part because they have data to use when making and marketing films, even if it's just data on their own past films.

One day we hope that real data is available to aid filmmakers and film investors and will, in my opinion, dramatically increase film investment and filmmaking quality that targets specific audiences. But until then, we work with the information we have. And it turns out, that's something.

Imagine a world where stock market prices were secret and the profits and losses of traders were secret. That's kind of like working in film. The only way to get insight into the best practices of trading would be to interview 50 successful traders and ask them their habits. If you did that and you started to hear the same ideas, the same habits and stories, then a picture of stock market success might start to emerge. You might find that the world is not completely resistant to analysis.

Even if you lack actual, objective data, we can make sense of the world through the lens of the experiences of a wide range of professionals. Not just one or two or five or ten, but if we interview three- or four-dozen professionals then maybe we get a level of confidence that we are getting a picture of the world as it is, and not only as we hope it to be. That is what I hope to do here. Create a picture of how the film world works from the combined wisdom of dozens of professionals that are living through it today.

Speaking of seeing the world as it is and not only through the rose-colored glasses of how we'd like it to be, next we'll tackle the issue of whether or not an artistic vision, bravely envisioned and expertly executed, will be the driving force behind our film's success. Can we make an uncompromising film – our film, our way – or must we compromise our vision to what will satisfy the fickle masses? Hint: it's not the good answer.

4 Fear and loathing
Commercial is a dirty word?

Commercially appealing film? Wash your mouth out with soap!

When you move outside the sales and distribution channels of film – and you begin talking to filmmakers, creatives, crew, writers and even some/ most producers – you get a distinct feeling that you are dealing with a group of people disconnected from the "business" side of the "film business." Although there is a growing number of writers, directors and other filmmakers that are becoming more savvy when it comes to the financial side of film results, as a whole, "creatives" are surprisingly uninformed and sometimes cavalierly unconcerned with the financial returns of a proposed film. It could well be how hard it is to get the information and how unreliable the data is on the finances, or maybe creative personnel just kind of give up.

Although my interest and focus was talking to film business professionals, I did interview a number of creative personnel. The idea of this research – to study how you make a film that makes money – seemed quite the novel concept among a large portion of the creative side of the industry. It was even met with a healthy dose of outright suspicion.

As a former tech entrepreneur who regularly studied the profit and loss statements for my company, it was enlightening how often I had to engage in a lengthy conversation regarding the value of this research when discussing it with folks outside the sales and distribution channels. Many film industry veterans were a bit perplexed regarding my obses-sion with having a film, you know, make money! "Why was *that* so important?" they would ask.

They would wax eloquent about how there were many different reasons to make a film and, you know, making money was only one reason. You might want to tell your story. You might want to build a resume. You might want the recognition. The accomplishment. Oh my, many different reasons.

I began reading sample investor prospectuses for film – there are several online. And although they stress the risks of investing in film, few of them will put forward the notion that the film is not a financial investment and focus primarily on the social benefits of making a film. Very few producers looking for investors would state that the primary purpose of this film was NOT to break-even but to build the resume of the filmmakers (on someone else's dime) or to win some awards. No. Most of the time, it seems to me, the filmmakers will start to ponder the artistic reasons they will make a film *after* they have secured the investment. Before they secure the investment, their top priority is making a good film and recouping their investment. Which is why such a large portion of a prospectus is dedicated to budgets, estimates, sales of comparable films, etc. I would love to see a prospectus that excludes all this information, asks for money but instead stresses the "intangible" benefits of having made a film. Although this prospectus might end up being more honest, I have not found one like this yet.

But the most interesting reason of all that industry professionals (outside sales) questioned my fixation in making a commercially viable film was quite a surprise: "Why don't you want to make a good film instead?" they would ask. Instead? "If you're going to spend so much time and energy on something, wouldn't you rather make something of quality and value instead of just some schlock?" one producer asked. This theme popped up enough throughout my conversations that I thought I should address it directly. The notion that kept coming up is this: there is ONE spectrum, which ranges from "good" on the one side and "commercial" on the other. Is this right? I don't think so. But I understand the misconception.

Even the Oscars, i.e. the Academy of Motion Picture Arts and Sciences, perpetuates this idea. The most commercial filmmakers of their age rarely are featured at the Oscars. Steven Spielberg didn't win an Oscar until he did a black and white film about the Holocaust. Commercially successful films that are good films often get nominated but almost never take home a statue. There were three *Lord of the Rings* films, each nominated for best picture but they didn't win until the third and final try, and it was largely seen as a composite award for the three films rather than just for the final installment. Comedians may win over audiences but they don't win Oscars. This fact is so well accepted that Will Ferrell lampooned it in a song he sang at the Oscars, ironically, in 2007: "Comedian at the Oscars" – Will sang: "A comedian at the

Oscars, the saddest man of all. Your movies might make millions but your name they'll never call!"

But don't get caught up in the myth that "good" is some kind of opposite to commercially successful. I encourage you to embrace the challenge of making your next film BOTH: a great story – and – commercially appealing. Tension, humor, thrills, chills, everything that makes your next film good can make it a commercial hit. Don't settle for solving just half the problem.

Francis Ford Coppola put sex appeal and action into *Apocalypse Now* because, as he said, he wanted people to go see it (he ended up cutting a gratuitous topless scenes from the final movie – but he did film it just in case). He was making a motion picture about the struggle to be good while being tempted to be evil. This universal theme would appeal to filmmakers world-wide but he also felt the need to solve that other dimension – what elements do I need to add to the film to attract the audience?

It seems it's easier to make a film commercially successful if it's also good. I would bet that commercially successful films are – more often than not – good films. Whereas I would assume a large number of commercial flops turn out to be lower quality fare. Thus your struggle to make your film a success with audiences is not so unrelated to the quality of the film. And if you would like to make your films commercially successful by fitting a specific formula that satisfies your audience like a horror or a faith-based genre film (two genres well known to be somehow impervious to bad reviews), then there is still nothing stopping you from making that genre of film "good."

Making a good film that no one sees is like painting a picture but not showing it to anyone. Get yourself an audience. The most reliable way to make a career in filmmaking is not to win Sundance (those odds are LONG), it's to make a film that makes more money than it costs. Do that once or twice and people will notice. Ask Jason Blum about that.

5 This stuff is complicated

One may be the loneliest number, but "profit" sure is the most complicated word in filmmaking.

I wasn't sure what to call this chapter. I must have changed the name of it four or five times. It was hard to create a title that walked the line between respect for all the partners of a filmmaker on the business side that are dedicated to helping filmmakers make money and make their investment back, while simultaneously stressing how the intricate, and often inefficient, network of companies in filmmaking have sometimes become an obstacle in doing just that. Chapter titles that I considered were: "The vast array of middlemen" but perhaps that was too harsh given the negativity associated with the term "middlemen"; or, "Your industry partners" but that doesn't communicate how the network of people who make their livings by helping films go out to the public have, through no fault of their own, become a particular kind of obstacle that stands stubbornly in the way of films and profitability. Just the size and complexity of the network of people and companies required to market and sell a film around the world is intimidating enough. And if you add to that the complicated financial arrangements that are made by these firms, you can see why filmmakers often throw up their hands and let other people deal with the accounting.

Groups like the Sundance Institute have encouraged filmmakers to "go it alone" and self-distribute and self-publicize. There is a feeling that many industry players are taking advantage of filmmakers rather than helping them to financial success. If not taking advantage, the feeling is they aren't helping filmmakers achieve the goal of financial independence.

The supply chain of the film production and distribution is dry, complicated and will strike most readers as outside the control of the filmmaker. It is not the fun creative work and it's not the rewarding, audience-building work, either. However, don't jump to conclusions of powerlessness. Education is power. The first step to changing the game is knowing the game is rigged against you. If more filmmakers understood these supply chain points, the industry would move faster to be fairer to the small filmmaker.

This is such an important point that I dedicate Part 3 of this book – "How films make money" – to making sure you understand the basic structure of film deals and film revenues. For now, I will summarize that small filmmakers are at a disadvantage in the marketplace for multiple reasons:

1. Filmmakers are paid last in the chain of revenues. Sales agents, distributors, publicists, aggregators, VOD platform, lawyers, theater chains are all entities that will take a cut of the film revenues before the investor and the filmmaker.
2. Filmmakers are not aware of what the standard deals are with sales agents and distributors and therefore don't know what alternative deals might best suit their film.
3. Filmmakers either never learn how the financial side of the industry works or they start to learn too late in the process.
4. Filmmakers prefer to walk away from a film once it's done, moving on to their next project – thus leaving the financial success of their creation to others.

There might have been a time when film revenues were generous and reliable so you didn't need to take an interest in the business side to make a good living as a filmmaker, but those times have passed. Times *have* changed and that's also our next topic of conversation.

6 Falling revenues

Falling demand for indies

The concept of supply and demand came up repeatedly in conversations with sales agents, distributors, lawyers, accountants and other industry personnel when talking about the challenges facing today's filmmakers. As I briefly mentioned before, the buyers are buying fewer films. Demand is sometimes staying the same and sometimes dropping depending on how much the buyer is making their own content.

Too much supply

On the front side of the supply/demand curve, the supply is skyrocketing. The filmmakers, due to the dropping costs of filmmaking, are making more – many more – films. Technology in the film space used to be quite archaic. There are video clips online of old-style film editing machines the size of refrigerators. And it physically cut the film inside the machine and glued it back together with the clips in a different order. These machines were so expensive and rare that you would have to rent time on one in your area. Editing alone was time-consuming and terribly expensive.

Now with the advent of high resolution, theater-quality digital cameras, the machine required now to edit a movie is: any old PC or Mac. All you need is some software that could be purchased for a few thousand dollars. And now – since the advent of the SAS (Software As a Service) online business model – this high-end film editing software can be rented, instead of bought for $21/month (Adobe Premiere Pro video and film editing). And since you only edit the film for the last few months of production, you can get away with all the non-labor editing costs of your film for less than $100. This is only one example of how film costs have dropped at an astounding rate. Costs haven't dropped linearly, they've dropped exponentially.

Falling revenues

Not long ago, Blockbuster Video and other video stores could be counted on for thousands of DVD sales, even for mediocre movies – thus the boom in the "straight-to-video" film market. Also, foreign markets could be counted on to "pre-buy" many films just based on a poster, title, cast list, genre and story idea.

A "pre-buy," also known as a "negative pickup," is when a distributor (usually, a foreign buyer) buys the movie prior to the movie even being finished. The pre-buy can happen at any point before a film is finished but it could happen before the film has been cast or prior to the beginning of shooting. Savvy film producers, like Roger Corman, have been able to sell films with little more than a finished poster and title. Then the funds from the pre-purchase can be used to pay for the production of the film itself. If a producer has secured enough pre-buys for a film then, hypothetically, a film might not need investors at all. All of its budget could be derived from loan, pre-buys and tax credits.

However, pre-buys have been reduced. DVD sales have dried up. Theatrical sales have gone way down especially for indies that are not some large franchise like Star Wars or Marvel.

I spoke with a film lawyer that some producers referred to as "legendary" in the business. Being a film lawyer made him a uniquely powerful voice since, with decades of experience, he was privy to audited revenue data from hundreds of client films over time. As a lawyer representing the interests of his clients and with the power to audit or sue if given suspect data, I knew his perspective would be a great reality-check for me. He said: "It used to be that 70% of your film revenues were domestic and 30% were foreign. Those numbers have flipped so now foreign sales are 70% of your film's take. And by the way, foreign sales have gone *down* over the years. That's right." He emphasized "The increase in percentage isn't because foreign has gone up, it's because domestic has gone *that* far down that even though foreign sales are lower, they make up now 70% of a film's total revenue. So you can do the math and see how far down total revenues have gone."

Next we talk about one of the tools a producer can use for the marketing and sale of their film – the festival circuit. A film's festival run can bring it accolades, free publicity, and if it wins awards, prestige and social proof. But the smartest producers know the limitations. Festivals are a vehicle. They are not the destination.

7 The downside of festival culture

I love the film festival culture and the whole festival eco-system that has come up over the last 25 years. It brings a growing and enthusiastic audience to films that may not be reached otherwise. It brings a support system and a sense of community to a very international and fragmented group of professionals that often are neglected. Film festivals bring hope and encouragement to featured filmmakers around the world when financial returns are not there yet. But (as a rule) they don't bring money back to the investors. Matter of fact, film festivals are usually a money-making venture by the organizers and fees for applications are often one of the primary revenue streams. Critics would say that some festivals are making money from filmmakers rather than for filmmakers.

If festivals reward good filmmaking or risky filmmaking that isn't commercially viable then they fulfill an important need in this creative industry. But if small festival attention dominates the consciousness of a filmmaker so much that they lose sight of opportunities to help their career then their record in helping filmmakers is more mixed.

As I have referenced before when many filmmakers were equating "commercial" with "bad," I wonder: why is it so hard for a filmmaker to wrap their mind around making a good, commercial film? Is it only the Oscars that have perpetuated the notion that commercial filmmaking cannot be award-winning filmmaking? Do festivals also ignore or denigrate commercial fare?

The number of film festivals in the world has exploded since the start of the Sundance Film Festival. Online film resources show the number of film festivals world-wide was around 3,000 in 2013. Today, FilmFreeway.com (an online aggregator of film festivals) gives us a total of over 8,400 festivals active in its database. A staggering number of festivals are now operating all over the US. The rise of the film festival culture is one of the most influential, yet under-rated, trends to hit the film industry. Other market-shifting phenomena have gotten a lot of attention – the drop in filmmaking costs, piracy, streaming video-on-demand, changes in consumer viewing habits – but the rise in film festivals has happened so slowly that the shift it has caused has gone mostly unnoticed.

But beware: one of the sales agents I interviewed had a cutting comment for those filmmakers fixated on succeeding through a festival run: "The festival world was created specifically to be mutually exclusive to commercial films. It was designed that way. It was a place to put films that had no commercial appeal." Festivals are working hard to make this statement less and less true each year. As festivals promote themselves, by extension, they promote the films in their festival and their festival winners.

Even though this agent's sentiment seems slightly outdated, it remains more true than untrue even now. Only a very few festivals (most of them international) got high marks from the professionals I interviewed as having any value to the financial prospects of a film. There are only a handful of festivals in the world that buyers will be present. Only in those festivals would a good showing result in boosted sales. If this agent is right, why do so many filmmakers believe it to be an entry point to the marketplace? Probably because of a few high-profile winners that come out each year. Thus, filmmakers think this is a way their small film can get on big screens and get noticed. Maybe they will be bought by a big studio, changing their lives forever.

Is that true? Mostly, no. The answer there is like asking, "Can you win millions buying a lottery ticket?" Technically, you can't answer that question with a categorical NO, because someone does win, eventually. But the answer is: Mostly, no. You can't. Between the reality of what a festival run can do for a film and what filmmakers expect from a festival run, is a large disconnect.

Just your chances of getting into Sundance have gone from 60% to 0.25%. Sundance is one of the oldest festivals and, currently, the most significant in the US. In addition to being a festival, a large number of buyers come to view the films and therefore it's one of the key film markets, as well. The presence of the buyers is what makes it so important to be featured there. In the early days – according to Sundance's website – there were 175 films applying to the festival and they showed some 125. Now? You have less than a 1 in 400 shot, if you bother to apply. At one point in the past, Sundance was so popular that the number of applications to the festival was often used as a rough estimate for the total number of independent films made in the US that year. Now you can no longer make that assumption. Most filmmakers no longer apply to Sundance, because of the long odds. Even though $85 is a nominal amount to apply to a festival, why waste the time and the $85? The, roughly, 4,000 feature films that apply to Sundance each year no longer come close to accounting for every indie made in the country.

Almost every film festival has awards and an awards ceremony. They often invite filmmakers to lead Q&A sessions before or after the film. They shower their filmmakers with attention and recognition. But do they shower their filmmakers with money? No. The filmmaker isn't in the festival circuit to monetize the actual festival run. Although monetizing the festival run of a film is possible, it's not lucrative.

The major way that a film festival run is monetized is by selling tickets to the festival showings. So there's a need to publicize the film at each festival and get the theater as full as possible. If a film plays 20 times in theaters throughout its festival run, and it plays to a sold-out audience each time, then that could be thousands of dollars going back to the filmmakers. However, it's not likely to generate substantial revenues that make the difference in a $1M budget film. The biggest, most important win for filmmakers in a festival run is a distribution deal with a studio or distributor. The question then becomes: how often does that happen? Same answers as: "Can you win millions buying lottery tickets?" Technically, yes. Realistically, the answer is a solid NO.

"There are only five film festivals in the world that matter to the value of a film," said one sales agent. Although he didn't tell me which ones he was talking about, I can say with some confidence four of them are: Sundance, Toronto, Berlin and Cannes. Maybe he was rounding up? Another distribution expert explained plainly why no one cares about films that get into some lowly festival.

She was talking about SXSW and Tribeca when she said:

> The quality of film there is low. The production values and thus the number of distributors there is very low. Sundance, Toronto and Cannes are the only festivals where good films are shown. Tribeca is a very small festival and SXSW you might get genre films there but again, usually no buyers are going there. The buyers only go to Toronto (first), Cannes and Sundance.

She was talking disparagingly about the two of the best known (and hardest to get into) film festivals in the country – festivals so hard to get into that most filmmakers won't waste their time and money applying and apparently, even if you do get in, no distributors will be there to buy your film anyway. Ok then.

The festival circuit thrives on having a few very high-profile winners. Those are usually found at Sundance. And then they are so widely publicized that everyone uses the availability heuristic to overestimate the odds that they can win one of these because they can so easily call to mind a concrete example of a winner.

> Availability heuristic – a mental shortcut that relies on immediate examples that come to a given person's mind when evaluating a specific topic, concept, method or decision.
> ("Thinking Fast and Slow" – Daniel Kahneman)

Winners at Sundance are easy to call to mind. They are splashed all over the headlines. *The Big Sick* won a $12M deal from Amazon in 2017, for example. The result is that everyone sees these films and believes this is the target. This is the type of movie that is "successful" at a festival. This is the big red dot at the center of the bullseye. Shoot for that. The problem is that Sundance is a uniquely American festival and the films are uniquely American. Many of these films won't sell in foreign markets and won't make any money outside the US. Even the comedies won't sell much outside the country.

The fact is that many in the film business know *The Big Sick* was the belle of the ball at Sundance in 2017. Fewer people talk about how many films sold for a (much more modest) profit at the American Film Market (AFM) in Santa Monica, the European Film Market (EFM) in Berlin, or Marche du Film in Cannes. These films markets don't get the big headlines, the Q&A sessions, nor is Robert Redford championing them. They are usually for more commercial films.

Both Sundance and the AFM are film markets where large numbers of film buyers shop for content. Sundance is incredibly hard to get in while AFM is not. Sundance is more like buying a lottery ticket. The AFM is more for working class, low-budget films looking to earn a fair profit for a fair day's work. If you want to shoot for the moon, apply to Sundance. If you want to play the odds, make a film for the buyers that attend the AFM in November in Santa Monica.

This is exactly the right time to talk about the next issue facing indie filmmakers: press. Sundance gets a lot of press. Most of the films being sold at the AFM have received next to zero and won't get much when they go out to distribution. Sundance gets a disproportionate level of attention because it gets a disproportionate level of press. Attention will work the same way for your film. You need to be the Sundance – you need to get a disproportionate level of press. If you want to beat the odds in the world of indie filmmaking, you need to get press to cover your film. But that's easier said than done.

8 Trends in film journalism

I once spoke to a talented writer/director that had kick started his career by making a buzzworthy film that showed in SXSW garnering attention and critical acclaim. With a strong festival and modest but successful theatrical run, I had anticipated a lot of press for the film but it had a paltry amount and only ten critics had reviewed the movie.

I was surprised by the response from the press so I asked him about the PR for film. I had the impression that once you have a quality film and objective recognition from a large festival, surely press would follow without much effort. But the process he described to me was essentially the same as it could have been in 1940 – i.e. to get press for your film, you need to show in the theaters in certain cities. Without playing in theaters, your film will get zero press, as both theory and practice both go. For the LA Times, Miami Herald, NY Times, San Francisco Chronicle, etc. you must play in Los Angeles, Miami, New York and San Francisco. These outlets only cover films playing in their cities.

To make things harder, all of these publications have minimum theatrical runs to qualify for a review. You can't just play one time in Detroit and expect the Detroit Free Press to review your film. They won't cover your film unless it's playing at least twice daily over some given number of days. Many publications in New York or Los Angeles require a run of a full week. Boston Globe requires five days. Houston Chronicle requires a four-day run. They all differ and knowing the requirements is important to getting your film press.

However, theater owners will not book an indie film unless the producers or distributors agree to pre-buy a large percentage of the seats which will reduce or eliminate the risk to the theater. If no one shows up for the movie, the theater owner doesn't mind because they have their fees from the filmmakers. If the showings sell out, then the filmmaker gets all their money back plus a split of the profits – but that's rare. It also puts all the pressure to publicize the film on the filmmaker. The filmmaker I spoke with about his buzzy SXSW thriller had to pay $15K for a New York theater to play his film for the New York minimum and roughly $10K to play in Los Angeles. Wow, what an expensive and risky way of gaining press.

Recently, another obstacle has come up. These city publications no longer guarantee they will cover your film even *with* the minimum requirement met. The New York Times had a long-standing guarantee that it would review every film playing in New York for a week. But not even the New York Times can support that commitment anymore. Too many films are playing for short stints around the city. More on this in later chapters.

I mentioned Project Lodestar (www.projectlodestar.org) before and they have done some interesting work running surveys on how budget cuts in film journalism affect independent films. In 2018, they published the results from two large scale surveys – one surveying film journalists directly and the other surveying film fans about their reading habits. These are some of their key findings.

Film journalism survey results

The Project Lodestar surveys showed downward trends in the industry of journalism in general and film journalism, by extension. They also show how these trends will be intertwined with, and negatively affect, small film in a disproportionate way.

1. Traditional newspapers, magazines and weeklies are employing fewer journalists across the US and that extends to film critics.

Every traditional journalist surveyed at a brick and mortar outlet like a magazine, daily newspaper or weekly reported cutbacks in budgets and staff (with the exception of the Washington Post). These outlets typically lay off their film critic and hire them back as a freelancer to pay them per review to cut costs.

I once sat down with long-time film critic from North Carolina, Matt Brunson, discussing how the trends in journalism had finally caught up to the city of Charlotte where he had been writing full time for the city's weekly paper, Creative Loafing, for decades. The city, just two years prior, had two full time film critics. Matt was at the weekly paper. And there was another for the Charlotte Observer, the daily paper. The Observer had laid off their film critic a year before, now only printing film reviews that it received cheaply through a Wire Service – i.e. reviews written at some central location and distributed to a large number of papers all around the country at minimal cost to the publisher. Thus the reviews had no direct correlation to what was actually playing in Charlotte. Some of the reviews were for films not available in Charlotte while other films actually playing in Charlotte had no review in the paper.

The cost cuts of the Charlotte daily portended a total shuttering of Creative Loafing in 2019, which leaves Charlotte – listed currently as the 17th largest city in the US – with no full-time film critic. While the Observer's long-time critic has fully retired, Matt continues to write about film on his blog The Film Frenzy (www.thefilmfrenzy.com). This pattern of salaried film writers moving to freelance and then writing for their own online outlet is a pattern repeated throughout the US, the UK, Australia and the world.

It is notable also that while many of these writers are pulled back into freelance relationships with the outlets that they used to work for, their paid assignments are normally reduced. The papers often are physically shrinking, leaving less room for column-inches dedicated to films, thus increasingly only the largest blockbusters get covered by the big city press. As stated previously, even the New York Times has reduced their commitment to small films. Once having guaranteed a review for every film playing a week in New York, they no longer make this commitment, leaving some films – even films with theatrical runs in New York – without any press coverage from the New York Times.

2. Most film critics report a reduction in the number of reviews they are hired to write but, strangely, an increase in the number of films playing theatrically in their cities.

The theatrical audiences for indie films have been decreasing for years. With the advent of streaming platforms to your home and boom in home theaters, people are choosing to watch many more films from their homes. Theaters have turned to value-add differentiators to attract an audience. They offer alcohol, dinner and waiter service. Lounge chairs with reclining features, and seat reservations are now all commonplace for a theater experience which wasn't true a decade ago. 3D films, massive digital sound systems that create immersive experiences, IMAX theaters and more draw people into theaters. But many of these features don't add the same value to a lower budget indie as they might for an intergalactic *Star Wars* film or the latest *Fast and Furious* film loaded with explosions and stunts.

The number of theater screens in this country has actually increased (marginally) – a few percent increase yearly. Largely this is the result of the growing multi-screen multiplex, not any increase in the number of small indie theaters. But while the number of screens increases, the number of theaters an average blockbuster consumes has dramatically increased. The #1 movie in 1998 was *Saving Private Ryan*, which opened on 2,463 screens. Compare that to *Avengers: Endgame* which opened on 4,662 screens in 2019. With many more theaters dedicated to the large blockbusters, you get fewer screens available to play small film.

The higher than expected number of films playing theatrically in any given city is, in all likelihood, not a result of an increase in demand for a diverse variety of films but rather a side effect of small indies playing shorter and shorter stints at each theater. Amazon and iTunes give preference to films that play a few days in theaters – i.e. giving those films preferential placement on those platforms. And in vying for this platform placement, films are developing the practice of playing just that minimum number of days in some set of cities. So whereas before, a theater might have showed two films a month, each for half the month – this same theater could now be playing four to eight films at far shorter durations. The result is that if your film is not playing in theaters then traditional press appears to be increasingly out of reach. Even if you do invest in short-stint theater runs, your film might still be passed over.

The rise of the film blogger

The only silver lining is the rise of the mid-range, online film "influencer" (otherwise known as journalist/critic/writer/blogger). There has been an explosion of film writers and bloggers across the internet that are not tied down to any particular geography. The "long tail" not only applies to films, but also books, music and now journalism.

> Long tail market dynamics – when a small number of popular products no longer dominates all purchasing. i.e. when the number of products available for purchase dramatically increases and purchasing is now spread across hundreds or thousands of products, each getting a small percentage of purchases. A short-tail business example would be a small bookstore where every purchase was driven to the small number of books available in the store. The infinite bookstore of the internet has made the long tail a reality in more and more industries. More products than ever are being purchased – in smaller and smaller quantities.

Film readers are not just reading the New York Times and the Hollywood Reporter anymore. Now there is an increasing number of film journals, each with its own loyal audience and each promoted by review aggregators.

Aggregators like Rotten Tomatoes have taken on the role of curating this explosion of film journalists and they have successfully ridden the wave of popularity of these writers. Film audiences are interested in the varied opinions of film writers and they have rewarded sites like Rotten Tomatoes with a large increase in daily traffic for the service they provide in curating a list of critics and showing a summary of what a wide range of critics (each vetted by the website) say about a film.

It is hypothetically possible for a filmmaker to reach a swath of these critics – that are unfettered by the constraints of writing only about theatrically run films in one particular geography – and to leverage this new population of film writers to gain traction in the press. More on that later on.

Now that we have mapped out the terrain and see where the rough waters and mountain ranges might be – we can start to document paths to get around all these obstacles. But before we start drawing up turn-by-turn directions, we better take a good look at the vehicles we will be riding in to take us to profitability. Get ready to kick the tires and smell the leather on the industry vehicles we are set to ride.

Part 3

How films make money

9   Rubber, meet road

I sat across from Carolina film director Edward at the offices he had set up for his production company. Edward was getting himself established for a career in film producing in the Carolina area. For this region, he was considered fairly accomplished since he actually had a film finished. He was a "made" and "sold" feature filmmaker. Even though this film had an ultra-low budget, still …

He has a full feature film on his resume: funded, written, edited, shot, scored, and, *sold*. You could watch it even – on Netflix, no less. We talked about progress he was making towards his second feature and the possibility of working together to make it. There was a script he had and wanted badly to direct. There were other concepts and ideas he was interested in and there were projects that he would do for deferred salary if they came together. He was looking for that big "high-wealth individual" to fund his script.

We also talked about his first film, the Netflix film. I was curious how the business side came together. Apparently, he was a disciple of the "just do it" philosophy and so I wondered, again, how that had turned out for him. He hadn't thought much about what he was going to do with that film until it was finished. So how did it get sold? Answer: he cold-called various sales agents. Nice. At least he knew to do that much! Shows initiative and gumption. Was he going to make enough money from it to pay his investors back? Answer: no way. Was he going to be able to use those investors on his next project? Answer: nope. Which distributor did he end up with? Answer concealed to protect the guilty. But let's just say: a large brand-name distribution firm that would end up taking most of the Netflix money in exchange for a vague feeling that that relationship would be of use to Edward in the future.

When Edward started the process of selling his film, he didn't know much about the business of film. In fact, that was why he made his first feature at such a low budget in the first place. "I made that film because

I wanted to learn that side of the business. I had worked behind the camera and even directed before but was never involved in the selling and distribution, so I wanted to learn that side of the business," he said.

That's an expensive way to learn film lessons, I thought. But my own efforts sort of bore out his frustrations. How long had I spent so far puzzling on these issues at that point? How much longer would I have to go? How do you learn this stuff if no one knows? Is the only way to learn about the mechanics of film finance just to make a film and experience it for yourself?

Fortunately, now you don't have to spend an entire year of your life making a micro-budget film and sell it to Hulu or Netflix just to get an idea of how the business works. Sit back and read this section. Reading a single chapter can't take a year. At least I hope not. And knowing the business side of film immediately puts you in the top tier of new filmmakers.

This section explains what happens to the film after it is done. It describes, in a nutshell, the "business" of film. Who the players are in the process, how each player makes money and when they get involved.

Edward didn't have the attitude that many filmmakers do: which is that the business side of film is just accounting and "I don't need to know that." It's not the rewarding part or the creative part, it's not even the logistically and intellectually challenging part of actually getting the film to final cut. The business side should really be taken care of by others, many would argue. But as a young filmmaker anxious to establish a career for himself, Edward knew that understanding the business of film wasn't just nerdy accounting. It was critical to any career as a professional filmmaker.

Marketing your running documentary to Nike customers?

Many of the filmmakers I talked to – as their film goes into marketing and promotion – talked a lot about the "target audience." If it's an environmental movie, they talk about environmental groups that might co-sponsor a local showing. If it's a documentary about marathon runners, they talk about partnering with Nike and finding running groups on Facebook. From what I can tell, real, professional producers never think this way. They look for "buyers" and buyers are not people buying a ticket to see your film.

For the purposes of this book and the purposes of the majority of your life in film, I want you to think of a buyer who is not a ticket-holder. A buyer is a distribution channel somewhere around the world – and those entities are, in turn, fundamentally responsible for monetizing the film by taking it directly to consumers in that region.

A buyer is a television station in France, American Airlines wanting to show your film in-flight, a theater chain in Germany, Showtime-US, or any one of thousands of platforms that show films to consumers and will therefore need to buy the rights to your film (hopefully) in order to have enough content to make their end customers happy. Your buyer could be Amazon Prime, Netflix, Mubi, HBO or some other Subscription Video On Demand (SVOD) platform.

Thus, selling a film can be less sexy than you might think – and in the small film world, a good bit more predictable. There is sometimes a feeling that film revenues are massively variable, incredibly complicated and incomprehensible. And this can be true. If you take the top films in the world into consideration, film revenues seem like a wild world too broad to wrap your head around and no one has much interest in trying. Perhaps it's these wild examples that keep most laymen (and even most filmmakers) away. But if you remove these outliers, the film sales business seems more predictable and boring. Many experienced producers I spoke with gave me the distinct impression that, very often, a film will have a value in the marketplace that's more narrow and predictable than a filmmaker might guess. With a solid understanding of what foreign buyers are buying and how much they are paying, you have a good idea of what your film will bring in, revenue-wise. And with that, you have a solid feeling of what budget you should not exceed if you want to be profitable.

For small films, film sales figures fall into an (often) narrow – and predictable – band. Let's go through the mechanics of how to monetize an average lower-budget film.

Film: a work of art is still a product

There has always been an uneasy duality between art and commerce. The question of whether a piece of art is a "product" – that is subject to laws of supply and demand – isn't even a question (yes, it is). The truism is less of a debate and more of an uncomfortable reality that many choose to ignore. A movie is a product with a fairly elaborate supply chain. Webster defines supply chain as the system of processes involved in the production and distribution of a product. Film goes from production to marketing to distribution to consumption – not all that different from a car or an iPhone.

The processes involved in the production and distribution of film have been stable for decades. Although processes and business models are starting to transform in response to new technologies, their slow speed of adaptation is bad news for indie film.

In other industries, you see parts of the chain being consolidated for efficiency. General Motors designs cars, manufactures cars, markets them and then has close partnerships, or outright owns the dealerships that sell them. Apple designs phones, manufactures and markets them, and owns the stores that sell direct to consumers. DELL computers revolutionized the computer industry in the 1980s by selling direct to consumers. Microsoft now sells directly. Chevron doesn't just sell gas at pumps, they pull the oil from the ground, refine it, and not only that, they research where else on earth there is likely to be more oil and they go buy or lease that land to drill for more oil.

These transformations that happened in the sales of cars, phones, computers and gas have not yet happened in film. Arguably, they are happening right now and until they stabilize, finding a profitable model will only happen with careful consideration and expert execution. The typical ways indie films were produced, sold, distributed and publicized are not working for the vast majority of indies, which is why this book is such a critical roadmap to a landscape so loaded with landmines.

10 The players

Let's walk through the standard structure of a film's sales and distribution supply chain and then talk about each party and get into details. Typically, as a filmmaker or film producer, you will end up with one or two sales agents selling your film. These agents will sell your film to distributors (i.e. buyers) both domestic and foreign. A distributor will normally represent a single country. The agents could end up selling "all media" (i.e. all rights to the film) to a distributor in one geography or just some rights (like theatrical or DVD or digital streaming). You can get money up front or just residuals – or both. There are many, many options. You could even do it all yourself (DIY) and not have any agents or distributors at all. Let's go through each step in the process, one player at a time.

Sales agent

The film sales agent is usually first in line. They are very much like a real estate agent, in that they usually work with a filmmaker for free until the sale is made then take their fees out of the revenues earned. They are a broker, providing value by connecting a filmmaker with the film buyer. They add some incremental value beyond that. For example, they could help you edit a new trailer for your film if your existing one is substandard. The same goes for your poster and even your film's title. The real estate agent is still a good analogy. A good real estate agent is going to tell you that you had better paint your house and clean it inside and outside. They might hire a professional photographer to take appealing pictures and pay a web developer to post your house on their website complete with an attractive layout. It's in their best interest to make your film more attractive to buyers.

A sales agent is commissioned at a rate of around 20% of the total film's revenues. And they often charge back to the filmmaker as much as $20K in expenses. More on agent/distributor recoupments later. However, despite the chunk they take out of a film's revenues, I have developed an appreciative view of services provided by sales agents. In fact, I think a good sales agent can be the indie filmmaker's best business partner.

Here, I'm only describing the logistics and the roles that each player plays. I'm going to get into the process of when and how to engage each one later. Later on, I will talk about the optimal time to begin a relationship with a sale agent – i.e. earlier than you probably think.

Like a real estate agent, there is no legal or moral requirement to use one. Many smaller festival films will not have one at all and will go looking for distributors (i.e. buyers) on their own. Also, much like a real estate agent, when you want to sell your house, you could have many sales agents trying to woo you because they want to sell your house/ film. They want to "represent" your film. They will send you (usually) projections or estimates which will tell you what they think your film will sell for in each territory. The territories are normally about 30–50 different countries and North America is usually broken out separately.

You must be very wary of such estimates since they are not binding and in fact, *some agents are motivated to NOT give you accurate figures.* If they give you accurate figures, say, that your film will gross a grand total of $150K in foreign sales, and another agent blows up the numbers to show you that they think your film will fetch $300K internationally, then you might go with the more optimistic sales agent, right? Even if, as it turns out, the more optimistic agent ends up getting you only $125K while the more realistic one could have gotten your film $175K. The point is, the logistics and incentive systems of filmmakers working with sales agents and getting estimates and picking an agent automatically lends itself to almost forcing agents to exaggerate. The most common rule of thumb (a rule I heard more than once) is: look at the estimates, which include a low figure (pessimistic) and a high figure (optimistic), take the low number, cut it in half, and that's about what you can expect from your film's revenues.

Let's summarize where we are. So far you have made a movie. You are being wooed by multiple sales agents. You get projections on your film's revenue potential in all territories. You engage with one agent domestically and another for foreign sales who takes 15–25% of the sale price(s). Now you sit back and watch the money roll in. The sales agent springs into action. They find distributors in each territory/country who will buy the film rights from you (as represented by your sales agent), roughly seven years. There is a lot of flexibility in this model. If you know that sales agent-X has many relationships with big buyers in

Europe, sales agent-Y has strong relationships in Asia and sales agent-Z has better relationships and a better rolodex of distributors in North and South America – then you are free to work with each sales agent exclusively on the territory they are good with. But it's more common to use one sales agent for all international distribution and, if anything, one more for North America distribution.

The distribution company

A distribution company is next in the chain of film sales and normally works within a single country. Not too many distribution companies I have worked with want your film for more than one country – except for Netflix. Remember, at this point, you just have a sales agent – working with you for free. You still don't have any money. A distributor is the entity responsible for actually monetizing the film in each territory. First, let's look at a foreign country. Your sales agent will likely (hopefully) sell your German film rights to a German distribution company for some dollar figure. Let's say it's for $15K. The German distributor, in turn, has relationships with German Broadcast TV networks, German theater chains, German DVD stores (if that's still a thing). The German distribution company knows it can sell your film to each of their buyers for a combined figure of more than $15K – none of these lower level details typically is any of your concern. Once you get your fee from each country, what happens in that country is typically not anything you care about. So you get $15K from Germany. And so on for each country/ territory. The US is usually an outlier since it's a more complex entity in most cases. You need a separate domestic distributor.

The lines between sales and distribution have been blurred by the changing marketplace for film. Perhaps when movie viewing was primarily a theatrical experience, the lines were clearer. The distributor put the film in theaters and collected the receipts, remitting profits back to the sales agents. Thus you had a very clear division of labor between sales and distribution. Distributors have relationships with theaters and spend money to get butts in seats. However, now that theatrical is such a small component of the movie viewing process, the distributor acts a lot like a sales agent, but just for that country. In fact, that's what a lot of distributors end up doing, simply brokering deals, in turn with sub-buyers like TV stations and DVD stores. But once again, this isn't too much of your concern at the foreign level. At the domestic level, your sales agent can help put you on Amazon Prime or iTunes – and therefore they are playing the role of distributor for the TVOD "window" or the Transactional Distribution Channel – more on windows later.

The formula

Distributors will almost always pay for a movie using a formula with three basic variables. The first variable is the "minimum guarantee." This is (or, better said, *used to be*) the amount the distributor *thought* your film was going to make you, in total. And in their infinite wisdom would mostly just give you that money up front and tell you: "so long!" and your assumption would be that they are the professionals and were right all along, take the money and run.

Therefore, in the old world, the minimum guarantee was a best guess on how much your film was going to make. If they overestimated, they would lose money, and if they underestimated, you and the distributor would split the overage after they send you the details of the revenues and costs of sales. The next variable is the "expense recoupment." These are the expenses they will charge against your film that they incurred in the selling and distribution process.

After expense recoupments and the minimum guarantee, the final component of many distribution payment models is the "percentage split formulas." Let's say you make a deal directly with Sam Goldwyn to distribute (i.e. "all rights") your film domestically. You and Goldwyn agree on a 30% commission, thus resulting in a 70/30 split in your favor. Now you can calculate your total film profits back from Sam Goldwyn based on the total revenues. Let's take an example.

Let's assume you have a fantastic film, and Sam Goldwyn agrees to pay you $500K in minimum guarantee. (By the way, this will *not* happen. You will never get $500K for your film but this is just an example so you understand the math.) Sam Goldwyn also has expenses of $30K and a 30% commission. If your film makes $1M in the US, how much does Sam Goldwyn owe you *now*? Easy. Remember, they have already paid you $500K and they have spent $30K in marketing for your film. So, they keep all of the first $530K – reimbursing themselves for the minimum guarantee and the expenses. Then from the remaining $470K, they pay you 70% or $329K.

The problem that distributors are having with minimum guarantees is that revenues are becoming too unpredictable (i.e. too low) and often a film is too risky to give any minimum guarantee at all. More often these days, a distributor will give a film a zero-dollar minimum guarantee and will pay the filmmaker a quarterly percentage out of the revenues.

More on the alternative deals that are starting to appear for indie filmmakers later on.

Concerning recoupments

Recouping costs in the sales and distribution process is a long-standing and reasonable practice. Theater owners will not pay you 100% of all ticket sales and therefore, obviously, the theater owner's cut should not be calculated into the sums paid back to filmmakers. Costs of manufacturing or delivering DVDs are hard costs to be deducted from the DVD sale price before calculating the profit of DVD sales. Marketing costs to get people to buy DVDs or theater tickets are often formidable and therefore recouping those sales costs also seems reasonable to some extent.

However, recoupments have been a source of ire among filmmakers because they have little to no control over them and they can appear arbitrarily high at times, coincidentally and suspiciously shrinking the so-called "film profits" to little or nothing. There are numerous anecdotal stories all over Hollywood about films that showed no "profit" at all. Hugh Grant was to be paid a percentage of the *Four Weddings and a Funeral* profits and to this day (Howard Stern interview) despite the hundreds of millions of dollars that film has taken in over the decades since its debut, apparently he has not been paid a dime. Apparently, all the revenues have been chewed up as costs – as unbelievable as that may be.

Filmmakers often think of these as hard costs associated specifically with their film, like the technology costs of encoding your film to iTunes and Amazon (maybe $2K per film) or the cost of manufacturing DVDs, or the costs of reworking your trailer for social media ads. Most filmmakers have a hard time arguing with those recoupments because those costs seem necessary, justified and benefit the filmmaker. However, Peter, a filmmaker whose $250K budget film was distributed through a major distributor for $0 minimum guarantee got a $30K expense deduction right off the top despite the fact that he knew going into the deal that they were not going to do anything with the film other than pitch it to Hulu for an SVOD deal, and put it on iTunes and Amazon TVOD. So what gives? I asked Peter where was the other $28K in expenses? After some research, I might now know.

Expense recoupments could be more about the distribution company's *overall* corporate expenses, not having anything to do with your film per se. For example, one possible way a large distribution company could calculate expenses in the sales or distribution of a film is to simply take their *entire* company payroll plus operational expenses, travel budgets, everything and simply divide it by the number of films they are distributing and withhold that amount in expenses from each film, each year. That's certainly a way to make sure the distribution company isn't going out of business. It pays all its expenses first, but, for a filmmaker that could be a bit unfair. Because each time the distributor buys drinks at the Beverly Hills Hotel bar, fly to Cannes Film Festival, and book the room at the Ritz, every filmmaker associated with that company is going to see an expense deduction from their film revenues.

And the small films are the ones getting hosed the worst because it's more than likely that the lion's share of those expenses, salaries and efforts at the distribution company are going to go to the bigger named movies in their catalogue. Typically, while at the Beverly Hills Hotel pool side bungalow, those distributors are going to be selling their latest Sundance winner with Ryan Gosling, not your low budget indie. When they fly to Cannes, they are going to be pushing the new Natalie Portman film they just got and not your film.

It's a sad state of affairs since most filmmakers will do almost anything to be associated with a large distributor. And yet, it seems financially that it's not beneficial at all. Filmmakers working with these big-name distributors get a $0 minimum guarantee, a lower percentage of the revenue split, and very high expense deductions.

Expenses deductions/recoupments are normally capped to some level nowadays but even that's not always true. If you don't read your distribution contract carefully, the expenses you reimburse your distributor – out of your film sales – could be variable or discretionary. Expenses deductions might not be absolute either – they could be recurring yearly. Film revenues have fallen but these deductions often have not corrected downward. Often these deductions eat up all the film revenues – meaning they keep all your film revenues and remit nothing to the filmmaker.

The other phenomenon to be concerned about when talking about expense recoupments is the rising case of the "film package." Over the years, sales agents and distributors are increasingly selling packages of films to buyers. These packages can contain ten films and the price paid by the buyer is often roughly the same amount they might have paid a decade ago for a single film. Sucks. The filmmakers are making 10% of what they used to make. Actually even less. Because the agents and distributors are *still* deducting the same expense recoupments from each film. The price might be amortized across ten films and the sales agent has amortized their costs across ten films, but they don't divide the expenses by ten. To be clearer, they might have paid for one ticket to an international film market, bought one set of drinks for the buyers and sold ten films. But they still charge each film the $20K in expenses. They just booked a $200K set of expenses against that package sale.

Thus I've seen the rising importance of expense reimbursements to the business model of sales agents and distributors. Distributors make most of their money from these expense reimbursements, even charging back their own time hourly to the films, like a lawyer would for legal work.

The buyer

The "end buyer" of a film used to be very simple. It was the consumer buying a ticket at a movie theater. The sales agent represented the film and "sold" it to a different distributor in each country and each distributor put the films in theaters in their country. Buyers were ticket-buyers. But that hasn't exclusively been true in a long, long time and for the smaller film with little or no theater presence, that isn't the slightest bit true. The end-buyer is the group buying it from a distributor. We could be talking about Blockbuster buying 50,000 DVDs of the film for their stores. Well scratch that idea. Doesn't happen anymore.

Examples of end buyers: could be a university wanting to buy your documentary or socially relevant narrative to be shown in whole or in part in their classrooms; American Airlines could buy your film to be shown in flight; Hilton Hotels to show your film in their hotel rooms; Showtime, HBO, Pay per view cable, Direct TV.

11 Monetization

Various rights to be sold

Thinking through the various rights that you are selling to a distributor and which you can keep or sell somewhere else is a high-stakes game of creativity. If you don't understand the potential payoff then ask George Lucas' billion-dollar bank account. In arguably the most famous case in Hollywood history of a filmmaker taking advantage of a creative use of rights, George Lucas decided he wanted to carve out the licensing rights for his movie Star Wars. At the time, Lucas didn't have the cachet he does now but licensing wasn't a "thing" back then, so when he asked the studios if he could keep the licensing rights for the movie, they thought nothing of agreeing. All they wanted was the rights to the theatrical run and the other more traditional lines of revenues. The rest, as they say, is history. Star Wars toys, comic books, action figures and games then made Lucas rich beyond his dreams.

The example is dated but it is illustrative. When sales agents sell the film to distributors, they aren't physically selling the movie, obviously. They are selling rights to monetize the film in specific ways. The most commonly discussed rights are theatrical revenues, TVOD, SVOD and DVD sales.

Other rights to think about: educational (i.e. rights given to educational institutions to use your film for educational purposes), hotels, airlines, cable TV and festival showing.

Windows without glass

A discussion of the varied rights available to monetize for a film wouldn't be complete without a discussion of the popular concept in film finance of windowing your release. Windows refer to the time windows that you make available for each form of film distribution. Typically, the first window is the 30, 60 or 90 days that the film could be in theaters. During this window, the common thinking is that it should be available in no other way. And therefore you want to drive as many viewers to see it in theaters as you can, thereby capturing the folks that most want to see the film and are willing to pay to see it in theaters.

As the thinking goes, after you have gotten your top tier audience to go to the theaters, next you make it available in DVD form for purchase, again trying to capitalize on the desire to see the film. Those viewers that want the film most will buy the DVD, even if they can't rent it. Then, after that, you can make the DVD available for rental through Redbox or some other small video store. Typically, whenever a DVD is rentable, it's also made available to "rent" digitally through Amazon or iTunes for $4.99 or whatever price. This window is called Transactional Video-on-demand or TVOD.

As time progresses, you make decisions on when to make the title available on airplanes, hotels, universities and all the other platforms. Typically, a Subscription VOD platform like Netflix or Hulu or Amazon Prime is one of the final windows to place your film. There is also the increasing popularity of Advertising funding VOD, or AVOD. This is for example, YouTube, where the viewer watches the film for free but must watch ads before and possibly during, thus compensating the filmmaker in some small way based on the number of times ads are displayed to viewers.

There is some research that indicates using the "desire/demand" model is incorrect when it comes to window-ing. In *Streaming, Sharing and Stealing*, Mahul Telang and Michael Smith believe that people that see a film in their home don't overlap with people that will see it in theaters. They also believe customers for different formats of books are not "all the same audience" – i.e. only differentiated by desire. They believe these customer bases will not cannibalize each other's markets. Their research indicates that those different formats are more likely conceptualized by consumers as completely different products than previously thought. Therefore those markets should be treated differently. Warning: this is still only an initial theory and although the research points in this direction, it's still pretty light.

If this theory is right, then it means the window-ing theory to delay availability on one format versus another isn't just incorrect but also harmful. It means that movies should be released on all formats simultaneously to take advantage of the initial marketing push. This has led film distributors to experiment with so-called, day-and-date releases, where the film is debuted in theaters and on streaming platforms on the exact same day. Again, using the theory that the audiences are not cannibalizing each other but are just different audiences so why not leverage all the press at the same time?

As of the writing of this book, there is not enough data to tell us if one approach or the other is more desirable and lucrative. We have discussed the difficulty getting real data in this business so it is not likely that a definitive answer based on a large sample size will be attainable in the foreseeable future. You will need to base your decisions on what your distributor and sales agent feel is best for your title.

Are theater runs possible anymore?

Theater runs are, to many filmmakers, the heart and soul of their dream distribution. Most filmmakers make their films to be seen on the big screen. They shoot the film with the thought that the cinematography will be enjoyed in front of a large audience and a big screen. Resigning yourself to the idea that your film will not be seen in theaters is a bitter pill that most filmmakers will not swallow without a fight.

There are other, less obvious, repercussions of a theater run that filmmakers should be aware of. First, theater runs will have a fairly strong impact on the press you receive. Although from my experience with "limited theater runs" in 2019, I have seen big problems getting these films covered by the traditional outlets in the cities. From anecdotal, non-scientific research, it appears that Los Angeles remains one of the only cities dedicated to getting traditional press to cover even the small run theater films. The Hollywood Reporter, Variety Magazine and other top-tier outlets continue to make an effort to cover the smaller film openings in Los Angeles. But who knows how long that will last because most other cities have reduced their coverage of small films, even those playing in theaters.

Second, a theater run is (perceived to be) an indication of quality. Many industry people have the perception that a VOD release is similar to the old "straight to DVD" release of yester-year. Some films would be on the shelves of Blockbuster Video without any run in theaters and you knew they weren't exactly an Oscar worthy production. This perception might not hold over time as Netflix and other streaming platforms make big budget productions with major stars and forego theaters, but it still seems persistent.

Third, the final repercussion is how a theater run might affect your subsequent VOD release. Platforms like iTunes usually give films "preferred placement" if they've played in some number of cities for some number of days. Movies that have played in theaters could also have their own, smaller, more selective, category. This has, as you might expect, spawned a new practice of playing in exactly that number of cities for exactly that minimum number of days. The hope is that the preferential placement on iTunes and other platforms will recoup the cost of the theater run, and more. The data on the success of this practice is also not yet available. When we do see some distributors release that information, we still don't know if the data can be trusted or if it is being exaggerated for marketing purposes.

The real question for theater runs is cost versus revenue. I did have the privilege of interviewing a company for this book that does nothing but take films to theaters. They typically take small-to-mid budget films out for theater runs around the country. The primary purpose of talking to the company was to get an indication of the difficulty of profitably executing a theater run for a small film. I wanted to know: Was it easy or hard? Were there ways of doing it smarter?

The owner didn't waste much time in disabusing me of the notion that a theater run could return a profit to the filmmakers. "It cannot," was the flat answer. Again, there may be exceptions but in a short conversation, he didn't want to mince words and waste time on a tiny sliver of outliers. Theater runs are incredibly expensive. For a "real" theater run, where you are playing a week or more in a substantial number of cities, the upfront cost is well over $100K most of the time. There is almost no chance of breaking even with ticket sales for independent film. Filmmakers wanting to go this route will have to view a theatrical run as a very large expense and must have some other reason for making this investment. It's an expense, period. And no business case was laid out that could make it a break-even. At least not today.

We should also note that this issue doesn't only stand for small-to-mid-budget films. Most data shows that the massive cost it takes to get people in cities to physically attend theater showings is roughly equal to the amounts the theaters are taking in, in terms of revenues. Therefore, the theory currently stands that most theater runs are often break-even propositions that work to promote the other film revenue streams. There are many people that believe Disney cartoons showing in theaters are loss-leads so Disney can sell princess merchandise in stores, tickets to Disneyland, Disney cruises and help drive consumers to all the other revenue streams that go with a successful franchise.

12 How much to DIY

Self-distribution movement (DIY)

The perception that distribution companies, sales agents and a whole host of industry support companies make too much money and charge too many expenses back to filmmakers has sparked a Do-It-Yourself (DIY) distribution movement. This means, you become a distributor and you monetize the film yourself – you promote it, get people to see it, find a buyer and collect the revenues directly. The benefits of managing the distribution of your own movie are trumpeted by many industry professionals but unfortunately too few of them turn out to be filmmakers. What you would have thought ten years ago was to be a *revolution* turned out to be a small protest parade. The revolution was planned. No one showed up.

There are prominent programs within respected organizations (i.e. Sundance Institute, among others) that have spearheaded efforts to help filmmakers self-distribute. However, many of these programs were terminated due to lack of interest. The reality is that distribution is a skillset that is diametrically opposed to filmmaking. The two occupations have different mind-sets. They sit on opposite sides of the brain but are dependent on each other.

It is unrealistic to ask so many filmmakers to take ownership over distributing their own films. Marketing and distribution is a calculated endeavor, using accounting skills, project management skills and requiring no small amount of mundane busywork. Pretty much the opposite of the kind of work that "creatives" – i.e. writers and directors – like to do.

There are additional, practical reasons the DIY model doesn't always work. Films take so long to prepare, shoot and finalize that if a filmmaker doesn't start their next project immediately, they could go years before making another film. Writers and directors want to move on quickly once a film is out and they want different staff to handle the marketing, coordination and sales of their effort. Although there are exceptions, from what I know of creative teams, they are not interested in marketing, sales and distribution.

This (understandable) reluctance to own the distribution, sales and publicity of their own film has led to the "managed-DIY" movement. Unlike, the full DIY movement, this movement has picked up some steam over time.

Managed-DIY

A new generation of distribution companies

Managed-DIY, sometimes called semi-DIY, or just a la carte distribution-as-a-service companies are popping up. Freestyle Media was one of the first to see the trend. With the plunge (or should I say, lack of predictability) in film revenues – both foreign and domestic – distributors began reducing the minimum guarantees they were willing to pay for films. At the same time, there was a dramatic increase in the films available to be distributed. The supply and demand curves flipped fast and hard. Risk-taking distribution firms that paid top dollar for movies went out of business – to be replaced with the new distributors – who pay $0 minimum guarantees. Distributors are now taking films with zero money guaranteed to the filmmaker.

This new generation of distribution companies, that do not pay minimum guarantees, is a business model built on volume and keeping expenses low. This model pushes more responsibility to the filmmakers and producers to provide many of the services that traditionally were the responsibility of the distributor. The business model goes like this: take on more and more films and withhold a smaller sum of expenses from each filmmaker. Then, either ask the producers to do the eliminated services themselves (like publicity) or charge the filmmaker an a la carte fee and the distributor can arrange for the service to be done.

In the old model, distribution companies withheld a large, possibly even a variable, amount of your film's first revenues. Now distribution companies are capping the expenses they recoup from your film's revenues. In some cases, they will commit to withholding *zero* expense recoupment at all, like Indie Rights in Los Angeles. With these distributors, they absorb the cost and risk of distributing your film online and you promote the film yourself. They could offer some guidance on how other filmmakers have successfully marketed their own films before, but they don't do it for you.

Other distributors offer publicity, promotion, even theatrical options to the filmmakers but it's an a la carte menu and the filmmaker must fund each option themselves. Previously, the entity fully responsible for monetizing the film, including publicity and marketing, was the distributor. Now the model is: distributors are providing fewer services, taking fewer financial risks, keeping costs down and putting much of the responsibility back on the filmmakers and producers.

13 Promotion and publicity – who's selling this thing, anyway?

Within this world of DIY and managed-DIY film distribution, the publicist's role is still in flux. Publicists remain locked in the old film business models of decades gone by. Film publicity is old-school. Many firms are quite long in the tooth. They often prefer the old ways – and that means publicizing old-school, theater films, playing across the country. This usually means studios films with big budgets. Those budgets (for publicity anyway) are still quite high so they can afford these same firms and pay the same fees they've been paying for decades.

Many publicists have the same 75 film journalists in their rolodex – i.e. the entertainment editors and salaried film critics at all the major newspapers and magazines around the country. These film critics are interested in major studio films which, of course, play in all the major cities. So the whole ecosystem still works the way it used to work. At least it does if you're talking about a major studio release playing in 100+ cities.

Few publicists want to – and almost none are prepared to – promote a VOD film that isn't playing in theaters but only streaming in iTunes or Amazon Prime. The critics who review these films are normally working on newly popular film websites like Film Threat, Film Inquiry, Film Daily or Movie Nation.

Thus, the indie filmmaker is often left in an awkward position for publicity. The distribution companies are scaling back publicity services. Theater runs (which make publicity easier) are out of reach financially. And the PR firms that normally do this work are too expensive and unlikely to be of much use anyway – unless you're playing in 100+ theaters.

To DIY your own publicity is a labor-intensive, time-intensive slog filled with rejection. Plus, since your film comes out on a particular date, the publicity (interviews, critical reviews and other articles) must be published close to that date. Trying to get a journalist to cover a film that came out a month ago is an even more monumental task because journalists have a hard enough time keeping up with the films that are currently coming to the public. In order to DIY your publicity, you must scale a giant learning curve, gather a huge rolodex of journalists and execute a sophisticated game plan – all under massive time-pressure. Even managed-DIY is challenged when it comes to PR because there are few, if any, real vendor options that a Freestyle, Indie Rights or Filmhub can introduce you to. Journalists are having a hard time keeping up with the major releases in their area and now they have to cover Netflix Originals, Amazon Prime Originals and Apple TV Originals. Good luck getting their attention.

The issue of publicity for indie film exposes a big hole in the process. I'm personally working in this space right now. Getting meaningful press for low-budget indies is one of the biggest obstacles between indies and getting an audience – which translates to dollars. With some technology behind the solution, there could be a way to identify journalists who write about small films. Film writers are your audience for promoting small VOD releases. There are no guaranteed solutions for this right now. No vendor can get your film a guaranteed audience. But progress is being made –more on this in the next part on solutions.

Part 4
Making profitable films

14 Sell the sizzle

There's an old saying in sales that goes something like this: "They might enjoy the steak, but they buy the sizzle." Filmmakers can make the best film ever made, but if they don't know how to sell it – nobody's gonna watch.

This universal truism – that applies to all products, not just film – was alluded to again and again in my conversations with agents, producers and distributors. But these experts often beat around the bush because it is an uncomfortable reality – an unpleasant one too. I felt often like these experts were trying to tell me some sad news that they had wished to spare me, as if they didn't want to be the one to tell me my cat had died or something. I had often gotten this odd sense that something was left unsaid in some of my conversations but after around 20 or 30 of these interviews, I finally dragged it out of one agent.

"I'm not sure if it's gonna surprise you or not, but when some TV network or one of these large Chinese buyers buys a group of ten films all at once at a film conference – shock – they don't watch the movies," one distributor said to me. It was like a light bulb went off. "How ridiculous of me," I thought. Of course, they don't watch the movies! Some of these buyers from China or Japan or Germany go to one of these markets and they have to buy 20 films in a three-day market. If they have to buy 20 films, then ideally how many should they watch before deciding on the top 20? 100? Are they watching 100 films and picking the top 20? Are they watching 30 films and picking the top 20? Are they even watching the 20 they buy? How are they making their buying decisions?

This is another reason that getting press for your film is so critical. Even if the buyers aren't watching the films, they will at least google your film or check out what Rotten Tomatoes is saying. What the film press is saying about your film could carry the day. When the film buyers are not watching your film, it leads to an even larger, more uncomfortable reality.

"Filmmakers always insist that their films are so good. But they seem to be missing my point. They don't realize that sometime the quality of the film doesn't matter," the distributor said. By now, I hope the reader understands why many of the interviewees requested to be off-the-record. Not many people want to be quoted as saying that "the quality of your film doesn't matter" and not many want to be quoted as saying that "large buyers of films don't watch the films." But that appears to be the general gist of the interviews. There is the *ideal* way things should work – when a television station watches 200 films and buys the best 20 – where quality is the only thing that matters. Then there is the reality.

But this concept shouldn't be so shocking. Isn't this just buyers exhibiting the same, exact behavior as potential viewers of your film? To a potential viewer, the quality of your film will only be truly assessed *after* they've purchased and viewed it. You need to convince them to watch your film with all the assets you bring to the marketing package – your poster, the cast you have wrangled, logline and the buzz you've garnered. The expert above is right. Quality is only important if you can convince them to buy the movie in the first place.

The entire process of development – casting, genre, story, etc. – concerns itself in large part with this question: How do you convince buyers to buy before they have seen the film? It's an astute question and it should accentuate in your mind the importance of all these, seemingly superficial, details. They aren't superficial. They are the substance of what's purchased. Quality is important to get them to buy your second movie. The sizzle is what they buy the first time.

15 Development

Crafting a commercial success

This will be obvious to some but it's worth a detailed discussion. To make a commercially, financially successful film, you will need to write a story that people want to see. And film it in ways that people want to watch. Then add elements to it that will motivate people to go see it and market it in ways that will catch people's attention.

The hero and the story

The topic of "story" came up often when talking to sales agents. What kind of story is it?

Story by Robert McKee tells us that there is a very good reason most "Hollywood stories" are structured the way they are. The Hollywood story is about a hero or heroine that is in a state of uneasy stability: an unhappy or restless static situation. Something happens, often out of the blue. There is an "inciting incident" that challenges the hero to take a journey of some kind out of their comfort zone. They *act*. They make their destiny happen. They confront obstacles, one after another – often with the help of an aged mentor or sage. They overcome each one. Almost always, they have one obstacle inside themselves. They have to learn a key lesson about life. They have to grow in some key way, change in some important way in order to overcome the final obstacles. In the end, the third act, they are tested to their very core. Often the mentor is gone by then and the hero must go the final stretch alone. All a part of the journey. They must overcome their greatest fears and prove they have changed. If they can, they win – changing not only themselves and everyone around them but the entire world. Luke Skywalker in *Star Wars*. Harry Potter. Tony Stark of *Iron Man*. All our heroes.

The story is this way because, according to McKee, we are that way. This is how we see ourselves and how we see the world. We see ourselves as the hero of our journey, facing obstacles, needing to overcome our greatest fears. We see ourselves as changing, most of the world remaining the same (to test us) and if we change, we can change the world. *The Hero's Journey* by Joseph Campbell wasn't meant to be a blueprint of the Hollywood picture – although it became that after George Lucas famously went on record as having read it while writing *Star Wars*. He meant it as a historical document recording the myths from all over the world that shaped how each culture sees themselves, others, and the universe. Without even really realizing it, he mapped human consciousness, a story that resonates with every person in every culture throughout time. Your plot should also resonate across cultures and across time. There should be universal themes and there should be thrills and charms that work anywhere.

Making sure your story has the universal appeal to carry it cross-culturally does not mean it has to be conventional and predictable. *Pulp Fiction* had unconventional dialogue, situations, characters, and even an unpredictable, quirky timeline. But its quirkiness belies a traditional hero's journey where the story of Jules's religious awakening and spiritual growth is the spine of the story. At the beginning of the film, Jules has an inciting incident of possibly supernatural intervention, and after some strange adventures his new faith is tested in the ultimate way – a test he passes by not killing the diner burglars but actually helping them. Tarantino puts Jules's final test as the emotional climax of the movie, taking place at the end, even though he must shift the timeline of the film to put it there. Therefore, he creates a heroic journey of spiritual awakening that appeals to everyone everywhere and places it within an otherwise very non-traditional script.

This is the reason the Hollywood story is this way. It is designed to connect with the hearts and minds of everyone who is hard-coded mentally to see the world from this first-person perspective.

After making sure your story has universal themes, genre is next question.

16 Genre

"When I try to sell a movie to any buyer, the first thing they ask is: What genre and who's in it?" said one sales agent.

It's a question that agents, in particular, are interested in since they are so focused on the foreign market value of the film. They get to look at dozens of films or more per week. They normally work with a film for free, getting paid a percentage of the revenue only out of the commission once they sell it. Perhaps because of this compensation structure, they choose films that they truly believe they can sell for something worth their time. They act as surrogate to the buyer and judge the film quickly, sometimes cruelly, like a foreign or TV buyer might. The same two pieces came up again and again in talking to them. And again. "It starts with genre and cast," said one sales agent. We'll get to cast later. Let's talk genre.

Genre is often the first decision any filmmaker makes about the film. We'll also go into why these are important. Genre is important because foreign sales are now so important. Each country buys the film separately. If the film sells in one foreign territory, likely it will sell in many of them. If it doesn't appeal to foreign audiences, you might not get any foreign sales at all. Thus, from a sales agent standpoint, you are giving away roughly 70% of your film's potential revenue if you make a film that doesn't appeal to foreign audiences.

When thinking of foreign audiences, you have to remember they could be getting a version with subtitles. The dialogue might not even come over word-for-word, but in summaries. The actor delivery of the line is irrelevant because it might be dubbed.

"Let the pictures tell the story," said one sales executive.

"My ideal film has hardly any dialogue at all in the first five minutes, the entire story is visual. And after those five minutes, I know what the film is going to be about," said a second.

"The biggest mistake a new filmmaker makes is the first 30 minutes are too slow and too talkie," said a third.

"A gunshot and a scream are the same in any language," said a fourth, referring to his two favorite genres of horror and action.

With the visual nature of the foreign buyer's tastes in mind and the notion that foreign sales might make up 70% or more of your film revenues, let's look at different genres and discuss how a small budget film in these genres might fare.

Comedies

One distributor said it best with comedies: "Filmmakers don't understand that even English-speaking countries have a different sense of humor than America. Often these comedies don't travel well even to England, Australia or New Zealand. They don't sell well, anywhere outside the US. And inside the US no one wants to see them if they don't have a star in them."

Particularly the romantic comedies came up again and again as a genre that *only* works if there's a recognizable star power. Audiences want to see an immediately identifiable and likeable male or female lead in a rom com.

Dramas

Dramas are the darlings of the festival circuit. They comprise the core program in most American festivals. In fact, the Sundance top award is simply called: "Dramatic Grand Jury Award." For the record, any narrative film could possibly win, even a comedy – they just don't. The other top award is for documentaries. The 2017 SXSW Audience winner was *Light of the Moon*. A drama about sexual assault. Heavy. Dramas can be powerful. They can change people's minds and their perceptions of the world. I don't think it's an exaggeration to say that a good drama can change the world. But the title of this book is not *Making Movies that Change the World*. It is *Making Movies Without Losing Money*. So, dramas can move slowly, be downers, have less than fulfilling endings, lack action, tension and suspense that will thrill audiences of all languages, and particularly be heavy with dialogue.

Comedies and dramas – the heart of any festival program – are two genres that make foreign sales very difficult and therefore put your film in a tough spot when it comes to that 70% of the film sales that come from foreign buyers. There are loads of exceptions and it's possible to hit the number and have your comedy or drama be a breakout hit around the world. But we have limited time here and we don't want to go too deep into exceptions. We want to stick the probabilities. The probabilities are lower in these two genres. If you are an experienced filmmaker with a track record, cast, funding and relationships that can get your film into foreign markets, you can make whatever film you want. If you are a first-time filmmaker or a filmmaker without a long track record of success, you need every advantage you can get. Including picking the best genre.

Thriller

Thrillers come up again and again as the top, most consistent genre. They play well in theaters internationally and domestically. They play well on TV. They play well everywhere. There are several large television buyers like Lifetime that will pay special attention to your film if it contains a female lead that is in some kind of dire situation and finds her way out in the third act. "Woman in peril" films are core programming in many TV markets that cater to female audiences like Lifetime, Hallmark and all their foreign counterparts.

Horror

There were mixed feelings about the horror genre when I spoke to sales agents and distributors. A few continue to feel like horror, rather than thrillers, is the top genre. But most believe horror was so popular 10–15 years ago that now it's been overdone. The market is oversaturated.

One good thing about horror is you don't need a star. In fact, many argue audiences want all their horror genre actors to be unknowns and expendable actors. Having a large star in your horror film could be detrimental to the audience's enjoyment because they will not feel the dread they crave – knowing that that character probably *will* survive until the end of the film.

Family entertainment

The next biggest genre mentioned to thriller and horror was family entertainment.

"What kind of picture would you most want to get right now from a young filmmaker?" I asked as I wrapped up one conversation. "Give me a girl and her pony! They sell overseas. They sell to television. Buyers can't get enough of them. Basically, filmmakers don't make enough girls and ponies."

Family entertainment is another instance of filmmakers not thinking enough in terms of supply and demand. The fact is the demand for this type of film is high all over the world. There are a lot of parents wanting something safe to turn on while they are out of the room. I know. I'm one of them. The quality of the film is not that important. It will find that audience regardless. And yet, on the supply side, I'm shocked at how many filmmakers turn up their nose at making films for kids. Look at Pixar. That studio didn't do half bad. Currently the largest entertainment Behemoth on the planet was started by a whistling, talking mouse. Making a film for kids doesn't mean that adults have to hate it. Pixar, in particular, is famous for jokes that the kids won't understand but the parents will. Making a Pixar movie is like thinking in two dimensions. The parents and the kids will need to be satisfied in different ways from watching the same movie. It's not easy to do. Yet it seems filmmakers don't want to make this kind of entertainment. They are more attracted to gritty drama.

And we go back again to the festival culture problem. There aren't a lot of Sundance and Tribeca award winners that have a dog or a pet monkey on the poster.

Family entertainment is also somewhat cast-proof. But it lends itself well to stunt casting, which we will talk about soon. In fact, it's easy to put a big-name actor as the dad or the mom or someone else that comes in and out of the film occasionally but doesn't need to be onset the entire shoot.

Documentaries

Not many sales agents discussed their work with documentaries. However, this has become an important genre because there is a nearly endless appetite for documentaries from buyers. And documentaries can be filmed, often, at much lower budgets than narrative scripted features with paid actors, writers, etc.

Bert Marcus, director and producer of acclaimed films like *The American Meme* and *Champs*, began his career in documentaries precisely because it was a good way to get into the film business. The lessons he's learned are similar to what's important in making a film of any genre. Getting well-known people in the film – and well-known music – is a part of making it commercially viable. Just like a narrative, your film must start by telling a story people want to hear and telling it in a unique way. Show a new side of a familiar story. Have that audience built-in by telling a story the audience knows half of already, and then tell them the other half.

Bert stressed the need for making not just a good documentary but a commercially viable documentary. "It's important to think about all aspects of your film before you even begin: music can make or break a movie – any movie. Music is critical to connecting with the audience and it's sometimes the most expensive part of a film," he says. What music can you get for your doc? How will you get musicians to give you the music for the film for less than what they would charge some large studio film? Who will be promoting your film on social media? Is someone involved with the film that has a social media following? Who will be available to walk the red carpet at the premiere?

The key lesson Bert tells new documentary filmmakers is not just to put celebrities in your film for the sake of it, but to tell a new story in a different way. You have a better chance of getting a celebrity in your film if you give them a chance to show the audience a new side of themselves. They get to talk directly to their fans and tell them what they want them to know without the normal filters. You're showing a side to the celebrity that the audience doesn't normally see. That's the key in both getting the celebrity in the first place and also getting the audience to watch.

17 Rising above genre

Indie filmmakers can take a lesson from Pixar and write a scene that kids can enjoy on one level while adults can appreciate them on a different level. Roger Corman is well known for making exploitative or otherwise outrageous, wild entertainment but he would always insist there be some meaningful "subtext" to his work. His films always had a message in them about the times he was living in, whether it be about McCarthyism, or the civil rights movement or some other social commentary. Value and meaning can be inserted in a film in many different ways. One of my favorite films, *Groundhog Day*, is funny enough to entertain almost any audience. However, it is the message about how one lives a good life that takes the film from everyday entertainment to timeless classic.

Thinking about genre more broadly

I spoke with Roger Corman's company, New Horizons, and there was the following epiphany: "Genre" doesn't have to mean thriller and horror. I looked at their website and saw a variety of commercial fare – one in particular that seemed like a low-budget remake of *Porky's*. My contact at Corman's company mentioned they make mostly "genre movies." Typically, you might hear the term "genre movie" referring to horror or maybe an action/thriller. I asked if the college sex-romp was considered "genre."

"Yeah, I think so. To us genre really is anything with a certain specific set of expectations from the audience. They are going to watch the film for a set of vicarious thrills, whatever they are. They have expectations and your job is to fulfill them. Fulfill the expectations that you set with your title, your posters, and your logline. And fulfill them not in a totally predictable way. If it's too predictable then they might not come back again for your next film. The expectations need to be fulfilled but in a slightly different way."

New Horizons takes the expectations set by the poster, the title and the logline (and the trailer) very seriously. Hint: so should you. Posters of *Death Race 2050* (2017) and *Death Race 2000* (1975) are remarkably similar. They have images of busty blondes with revealing outfits, cars speeding by, fire, explosions and (in the former) ray guns and machine guns. *Slumber Party Massacre* (1982) and *Slumber Party Massacre 3* (1990) also look similar. Both have not one or two but three and four scantily clad young, frightened girls fearing for their lives, trapped while a psycho-killer approaches. For Freudian imagery, in both posters, the male killer approaches with a drill held between his legs. Subtle, these posters are not. Movie-goers know that, for this film, they are going to see barely-dressed college girls getting chased around by psychos with chain-saws or whatever.

The poster, title and logline set an expectation in the mind of the audience which must be fulfilled. Remember the "shocking truth about buyers" – i.e. that they often don't watch the movie? How do they make their buying decisions? From the expectations set in the poster, trailer, logline, genre and cast.

Set up expectations to sell the film to the audience but don't set false expectation. Unfulfilled expectations would lead the viewer to disappointment, even if the overall quality of the film is strong. If you want your audience to be surprised by plot twists then save a few for the film without revealing them all in the trailer. If you want your audience thinking the film was funnier than they expected it would be, then don't put all the funniest gags in the trailer.

Expectations and the press

It is said that Roger Ebert revolutionized film criticism and I don't think that's an exaggeration. He understood that to be influential, he had to be famous. He had to reach audiences. He went to television when the vast majority of his peers – even today – prefer to stick to the printed page. When he created his show, he knew to partner with Gene Siskel to show conflict for the audience when they disagreed and camaraderie when they agreed. They would go on the Tonight Show to yuck it up with Johnny Carson. And they walked the red carpet at the Oscars alongside the celebrities whose films they critiqued. But Ebert changed film criticism not just out of showmanship but the content of his reviews.

Prior to Roger Ebert, arguably, films were judged against the same yardstick. There was a hypothetical "ideal film" and all films were judged against this standard. If you weren't aiming at being that kind of film, then you were automatically going to be panned by most critics. At the very least, you were being inadequately ambitious. Ebert did not judge films this way. To him, he would always assess what the film was "trying to do." He then judged it purely on whether it succeeded in achieving its own goals. A modest film with modest ambitions could earn praise from Ebert if it did just that little bit plus a small amount more. A horror film would earn a positive review if it was scary, and that's it.

Ebert's style of review is now the norm. This style has also become more popular because the number of films has scaled so dramatically. The budgets films work with are now skewed from $0 to hundreds of millions of dollars. And so we find ourselves in this same old position. The expectation you set with the poster, logline and cast not only affects who will buy your film but it will also affect how a critic will judge your film. Do not set the expectation that your film will rival *Titanic* as an accurate period piece set aboard a cruise ship from the 1900s when your budget and period details are modest.

If you filmed without a script, make sure to say so somewhere in your material. If you filmed without professional actors, get that out there before people watch. If the entire shooting schedule was just seven days, mention it, discreetly. There is a fine line, of course. Setting expectations too low might cause people to skip your film altogether. These are the high-wire acts that an indie filmmaker must continually perform to be successful.

18 More film elements

Nudity

Some folks I interviewed jumped to the conclusion that nudity would play a key role in a commercial film but I found little evidence for that in my research. Because of the dominant role of television and foreign sales to these lower budget films, many sales agents and distributors stressed the importance of downplaying nudity. Many foreign markets in the Middle East and Asia would simply not buy films that had full nudity. Obviously, many television markets would frown on nudity.

One sales agent had the best tip: "Make sure your nudity happens in very contained areas, easy to edit out. That's the goal. Make sure no major plot points happen during a nude scene. No critical dialogue happens during a nude scene. The ideal nude scene is easily edited out and doesn't change the movie."

Going back to Roger Corman: Director Francisco Menéndez gave an online interview about his film with Corman, *Stealing Las Vegas*, which proves to be an illuminating case study. That film follows the formulas set forth in this book to a tee. Ultra low budget of $250K. $50K of which went to Eric Roberts who played one of the bad guys. The leads were new, young actors and Eric is the bigger name actor with appeal to foreign buyers that only needs to be onset for a short time (see the stunt casting section later on). Menendez recounts how they were set to film a scene in a strip club and he misinterpreted Corman's instructions. Menendez, in the only scene in the movie where he could have placed gratuitous nudity, told the actresses they could keep their tops on. He later regretted this decision.

Once the film was done, Corman watched the film and asked: "Where's the nude scene?" Menendez then had to pull the cast back together for another day to shoot the strip club scene again – topless. Without a doubt, this nude scene is completely superfluous. It probably contains no critical story lines nor dialogue and is easily edited out of the film, if necessary for certain buyers. The takeaway is to get a nude scene if you feel like your buyers might be interested. But make sure it's easy to edit out.

Violence and blood

Another common misconception is that going overboard on violence and blood is a ticket to commercial success. I did speak with some agents that specialize in "blood and boobs" films but most expressed hesitance and a dissatisfaction of too much blood. One European agent expressed disapproval, saying that Americans didn't understand that many other cultures are more sensitive to nudity and violence and less liberal in their tastes. They want more restrained entertainment.

When discussing the balance of violence and blood in film, the movie *Get Out* (2017) often came up in conversation. Across the board, sales agents and distributors salivated over the film's balance. Spooky without being bloody. Scary without being overly violent. After watching *Get Out*, I was shocked that it had warranted a horror genre classification. I considered it more of a thriller but that's the balancing act. Have the benefits of being called "horror" but none of the downside and the risk.

Television is playing a bigger role in buying small films these days. Excessive blood and violence will hurt your film when it comes to marketing to TV buyers.

19 Drafting

Drafting in filmmaking means you are designing your film to have elements in it that are already familiar to your target audience. It should look in some way familiar, thus some of the hard (and expensive) work to create audience interest is groundwork already laid by previous stories or films. There are many, many ways of "drafting" from familiar concepts. Some industry professionals believe drafting is a sub-concept of an overall goal of "audience familiarity." In other words, making sure that the audience has a sense of familiarity with your film before they even see it. Music often has the same goal. A song should sound familiar without being too similar to something else.

Let's review several different ways you can have your film take advantage of drafting so you plug into an audience that's already predisposed to be interested in your film. Drafting is similar to stunt casting (discussed later), in that an amateur filmmaker might turn their nose up at the technique. The amateur might think it's overly commercial or a "short cut" to an audience without realizing that big-league filmmakers use the technique all the time.

There are gratuitous examples of drafting that might cross the line of good taste or even copyright infringement. Mockbusters, for example, are films expressly created with the intention to exploit the publicity generated by another film by very explicitly mimicking their posters, marketing, even to the point of creating titles that sound similar to the original. If you intend to draft *that* closely to some existing large, successful film, you better get sound legal advice. There have been many lawsuits from plaintiffs like Disney and Warner Brothers, suing when smaller studios created "knock-off" movies that looked too similar to the original. Most of these lawsuits were ultimately unsuccessful but when in doubt, get a lawyer.

Big time studios draft all the time. What's a sequel, if it's not drafting off the original film? The Marvel sequence of movies have been the massive hits in part because of the innovative way they draft off prior films. Their key achievement is in creating an entirely new way of drafting, i.e. place the films in the same "Universe" and have the main characters in one film be supporting characters in other films. Genius. Drafting without sequels.

Don't you wonder about the spate of films having come out recently all "based on the novel." Drafting on a novel works on multiple levels – first, there's a built-in audience of target viewers (i.e. the people that read the book). Second, the story-line and plot have been proven out to be strong. And third, the "based on a novel" serves as a "social proof." Even to those that haven't read the book, hopefully they think: "if it's a successful book, then must be good."

The list of literature, characters and stories that are in the public domain might surprise and delight a first-time filmmaker. You can make your own Sherlock Holmes movies with no fear of copyright infringement. Shakespeare has a rich body of work that can be copied outright or it can be mimicked with stories that are "based on" this play or that play. You can make a sequel to Romeo and Juliet, but you might have to change the ending so the main two characters live!

Again, you can look no further than the behemoth themselves – Disney. Not only do they *still* do drafting – in fact, inventing a new kind of drafting – but they had foundational success based on drafting. Do you think Snow White is a Disney character and story? It is not. Disney lifted the story from a 19th-century fairytale by the Brothers Grimm. The story is complete with seven dwarfs, a magic mirror, poisoned apples and an evil queen. Again, don't turn your nose up at these techniques.

List of concepts that are in the public domain: The Bible, The Buddha, The Koran, The Torah, Shakespeare, Sherlock Holmes, H.P. Lovecraft, Edgar Allen Poe, Joan of Arc, Grimms Fairytales, Jane Austen, Charles Dickens, Mark Twain, etc.

Drafting can also help you with drawing cast and drawing investment. Telling an actor they will play Sherlock Holmes, or an actress they will read lines from Romeo and Juliet is preferable perhaps to some of the scripts they are sent.

To some degree, making a World War II story – or any story where Nazis are the bad guys – is a form of drafting off of "bad guys" already in the public domain. And World War II stories famously sell fabulously throughout Europe.

Apocalypse Now was not an original story either. The screenplay was based on *Heart of Darkness*, the Joseph Conrad book written in 1899, now in the public domain. Coppola's Oscars – *Godfather* and *Godfather 2* – were both based on a novel.

20 Casting

Jeanette B. Milio, a producer that also teaches Film Finance at UCLA, stresses my current topic's importance: "I tell my students there's three things that is important when selling your film: Cast. Cast. And Cast."

Cast is the dominant topic when the sales agent, distributor or anyone talks about the commercial viability of a film. And with the plethora of films coming out, cast is set to take a bigger and bigger role. "Get someone in it!" cries Suzanne Lyons author of *Indie Film Producing*. "Be smart. Put someone in your movie. It doesn't have to be Tom Cruise but someone that will help sell the movie."

"That's easier said than done," said Edward, my Carolina filmmaker friend as we were discussing the best approach to get bankable cast for his next film idea. I explained his need to get someone in his southern drama in order for the film to be worth anything. Edward has a lot of company in thinking that casting a name actor in your film is just wishful thinking. The attitude that it's not legitimately doable is the first challenge of getting someone in your film that brings value to the production.

There is a general rule among producers, distributors and agents that they would recommend would-be filmmakers to follow. It goes something like this: take your $250K movie. But instead of spending $250K, make your movie for $200K and spend $50K on a star to come in for a week onset and play a small role. Now you have a $200K film (with a star in it) instead of a $250K movie (without a star in it). I guarantee you, the $200K movie is worth far more (in every market) than the $250K movie.

"Budget doesn't matter anymore," says a sales agent that has turned his company into a production company as well as sales. "Now you can, you *must*, make a movie for $250K that *looks* like a $2.5M movie. Production value has to be so high and you can do it with these technologies but when you want your movie to *look* like $2.5M then you *have* to get someone in it. If you want to look like a heavy-weight movie, get stars in it that will make your $250K movie look like a $2.5M movie!" Remember when I said that all filmmakers and producers want you to think their film has a budget of 2–3 times what it really was? Well casting is a big part of making that happen. A film's perceived budget goes way up if you can get well-known actors in it.

One of the questions I was hoping to get answered from all my research is *who* needs to be in your film to make it appealing to buyers – foreign and domestic. Which cast is worth the money and which is not? *Who* do I need to get to sell a film? Is it Eric Roberts or Michael Madsen? Who has cachet in the markets these days? I did get a lot of input on this but generally the answer was: you should check in with a sales agent once per quarter or twice per year because it changes every year. A few years ago, Steven Seagal was hot. For a while, it was Michael Madsen and Eric Roberts but they have done so many movies in the last few years that they have diluted their value. If you're talking to a European buyer that's already bought two Eric Roberts' films this year then they might take a pass on yours, giving you a zero in that column. If Eric takes a long vacation and hasn't done a film in a while, by the time you're reading this, he might be in demand again. The perfect candidate for stunt casting is someone that is currently being ignored by the bigger studios with the bigger budgets but has name recognition around the world – possibly from years past. And if they have a TV show in syndication in foreign territories, all the better. Luke Perry in *Black Beauty* (2015) was a great example of a well done film that sold very well in an otherwise slow film-sales year.

Moneyballing your cast

Moneyball is Michael Lewis' 2003 book on how Billy Bean of the Oakland A's – one of the poorest baseball franchises in the league – bucked all the traditions of recruiting baseball players to build teams that consistently outperformed teams with much larger budgets. The theory is that there are inefficiencies in the baseball salary market. That means that some players demand huge salaries disproportionate to the true value they bring to the team. Skills like stealing bases, running fast, diving catches might put a player on the evening news highlights and drive up their value in the market without helping their team win very much. Other players, that have a penchant for fouling off numerous pitches, not swinging at bad pitches, etc., therefore, drawing a lot of walks – could be cheap to bring on your team. Stacking your team with these cheap players (that generate runs) turns out to be a great way to win ball games without spending much money.

There is an analogy to film. There are actors in the market that are cheaper to hire than they should be based on the value they bring to a film. It's your job – as filmmaker or budding producer – to find them. An actor might have had a successful TV series ten years ago and hasn't worked all that much since. But if that TV series happens to be in syndication all over Asia and Europe right now, their face on a poster could be recognizable enough to guarantee those foreign buyers will break their piggy banks to get your film. And that TV actor might just be chomping at the bit to take on a beefy roll in a film even for a lower fee.

Moneyballing your cast usually involves at least some of the following.

Stunt casting

Stunt casting is the process of casting a "name" actor in a role that does not require a lot of time from them. Actors normally make a specific amount per day on the shoot. Reducing the number of days the big actor is on set is beneficial to both actor and filmmaker. It's attractive to the talent in the first place (they are more likely to say "yes" if it's a smaller time commitment) and it keeps the cost of the big star down. Plus, there's the added, hidden costs of having a star on set. You might need to hire a better makeup or hair person for the star. You will probably not be able to put them up at Motel 6 like everyone else. There are costs in having a star on your set that are above and beyond the price you are paying the star. Therefore, with stunt casting, get a big name star on set for 5–10 days, max.

There are some rules to not screwing up stunt casting. One producer said that the star should be onscreen for, at least, 20–25 minutes. Another distributor commented that there is an art to stunt casting because you want the star in the beginning, the middle and the end of the movie. You want to make it feel like they are all over the movie. But they can't be in every scene or carry the weight of the narrative since that would require them on set too much. The adversary or the bad guy is often a good choice for the star. They come in at the beginning, appear occasionally throughout, and they are often in the climactic scenes at the end.

If it's good enough for a two-time Oscar winner

One of the greatest documentaries you can rent about filmmaking is *Hearts of Darkness – a Filmmaker's Apocalypse*. The film is about the making of *Apocalypse Now* by Francis Ford Coppola. The documentary is largely based on the audio and written journals of his wife, Eleanor Coppola. The 1979 film was a massive critical and commercial success but it wasn't until 12 years later, in 1991, that the documentary came out.

When he made *Apocalypse Now*, Coppola already had two Oscars on his shelf for the *Godfather* movies. And yet, watching him in action, you see that casting Marlon Brando as Kurtz was a genius example of stunt casting. It fit the model exactly. He offered Brando what would now be called a "pay or play offer" of $3M for just 20 days of shooting. For context, principal photography on the film was 15 months. Nonetheless, Brando's picture was front and center on the poster and his name was above the title on several of the first posters. Martin Sheen, on the other hand, was a relative unknown. Sheen was in nearly every scene, carried the narrative, and was the main character, Willard. Marlon Brando was mostly featured in the final, climatic scenes. However, there were photos and recordings of his voice played in the beginning of the movie as well, so his presence is felt even early in the film.

Seeing Coppola stunt cast his bad guy is an enlightening lesson that these tools work. They work for first time filmmakers and two-time Oscar winners.

Rule #1 of stunt casting: it's possible

The first trick to successful stunt casting is just knowing it's possible. That was a theme that kept coming up.

"How do you get someone that has value in your picture? That's the trick, right? How do you get them?" I asked.

"Oh, filmmakers would be *very* surprised how, um, 'getable,' a lot of these stars are," says one distribution company that distributes a lot of mid-tier and low-budget films in the US. "In particular, that pay differential that you hear a lot of actresses complaining about? That's real and while it persists, filmmakers should be aware of it. Hire actresses! You'd be surprised how well known of an actress you can get for very little money," "Very little money," of course, is relative. Stars are well paid, per day.

"How do you get a name actor or actress?" I asked.

"If you send an agent an offer with *any* money attached," said one film consultant. "Even $1. They have to – legally – send that offer to the actor. They can't just throw away your script. They need to give the offer and the script to the actor or actress. Actors want to work. That's what they do. They want jobs. They especially want to do something they haven't done a lot of already. Be smart. Offer them something they might actually *want* to do."

"We got X actress by offering her a romantic comedy role. She was tired of being the femme fatale in a thriller. She wanted to play someone that everyone was rooting for and everyone wants to be friends with in something light hearted," says a producer responsible for the casting of a low budget film that did some stunt casting in a key role.

"You'd be shocked. We paid Y actress $500K for a movie eight years ago and now you can get her for $10K. Don't say the actress name but that's not unusual," said another producer.

Rule #2: the pay or play offer

Use a pay or play offers. A pay or play offer is a hard offer of money to an actor or actress as soon as they accept the part. "They work," says a successful Canadian producer that makes all their films in Canada with financial support from the government. When the money actually changes hands is negotiable. However, the commitment to pay them *whether or not* the movie is ever made happens immediately upon them accepting. Usually there is a date-range set. You are offering to pay them for 1–2 weeks of work in, say, August. $5K per day. Ten days, $50K. If they accept, they get paid whether or not the movie is a *go*. These offers work but obviously you need to be certain your movie is a go and you have the money.

Making a pay or play offer work can be a lot about the negotiation. These offers can absolutely be conditional. They can be conditioned upon getting the film fully funded. In these instances, your investors aren't risking the entire sum paid to the actor but they usually risk something. Often, in these offers, the agent will need some percentage, say 10–15% paid as a holding fee and the rest is paid upon the date in question. The remaining sum can be contingent upon funding or some other "out" that the producer has. But some of these funds will be at risk, which is why getting most of your funding first is, by far, the better strategy.

Rule #3: balancing act

There is an interesting balancing act for a producer between casting and the monetization of the film. On the one hand, your buyer will want a specific actor in a specific role that the market wants to see them in. In other words, the market wants your actor in a role that is stereotypically theirs. They want Eric Roberts in a thriller. Sharon Stone as a femme fatale. "Get Sharon Stone as your femme fatale and I'll sell it to every territory in the world."

But the problem is, to *actually get* Sharon Stone, you want to offer her something different – something she doesn't usually do. Something she'll work for less money to do. Therefore, to get them, you put them in a role that makes it harder to market them. I would advise you not get lazy or cut corners with regards to marketing. Remember, how you market the film dictates the expectations of the viewers and buyers. If you don't market the film and its stars in the right way, you get an *Everything Must Go* problem. I'm sure getting Will Ferrell for the role was made easier by the fact that he was attracted to a dramatic role (for a change). But that made the producer's job harder in marketing the film. The producers decided to short-cut their marketing dilemma and simply promoted the film as if it were a comedy which, in retrospect, was probably unwise.

Rule #4: get a producer that can pull it off

Find a producer that has worked successfully with some cast at the level that you want. Even if they aren't the main producer, you can pay them a co-producer fee if they bring important cast. There are casting agents that are looking to move into a producer role. Offering them an associate producer credit if they can arrange valuable cast is a good method to get them to work with you initially without a fee. An associate producer credit could come with a fee (once the project is funded) or simply help them launch into a new line of work.

Rule #5: get more than one

As one producer I spoke with put it: "You should cast: A) one social media star that's never made a movie – someone with 4 million followers on YouTube so they will promote your film for nothing; B) get an older TV star that's in syndication maybe in foreign territories; C) get a WWE wrestler because that's all of middle America; D) get someone that resonates with the Lifetime channel or whomever you think is your backup buyer."

Another successful director I spoke with uses a three-part formula in casting. First, the lead, isn't usually the biggest star. They will need to carry the weight of the narrative and are in most scenes. Second, stunt-cast-A can be the villain or some other important character that is in the beginning and end of the film. Third, the director often plans a stunt-cast-B who's just on-set for a single day but not just a cameo. The second stunt cast will be in multiple scenes and can be lower down on the casting sheet so no one expects them to be all over the film.

Moneyball was about building a full team. Get a set of talent that can all bring value to the production. *Ashley* (2013) producer Tom Malloy pulled established talent, a social media personality and TV syndication talent together. Michael Madsen was the biggest star in the film, and only had to come to set one day. Jennifer Taylor was an established actress in syndication all over the world for her role in *Two and a Half Men*. Nicole Arianna Fox had a large social media following and had just won *America's Top Model*. You don't have to put all your eggs in one basket in terms of star-power.

21 Producers and producing

There is a great story from *When We Were Kings*, a documentary about the 1974 fight between George Foreman and Muhammad Ali. It's not a story about making a film but it might as well have been. Putting on a fight turns out to be similar to making a film in that you need money to get the talent to put on a boxing match just like you need money for talent to make a film. Famed sports writer, Thomas Hauser, looked right into the camera and told a story about how Don King brought the fight together. People wanted to see the fight. No one could arrange it. How would Don King put it all together?

"Don King had Muhammad Ali's signature on a piece of paper that he would fight George Foreman for $5M," Hauser tells the camera. At that time, $5M was an outrageous sum for a fighter and probably wasn't hard to get Ali's agreement to a fight for such a crazy sum. "Don King also had George Foreman's signature on a piece of paper that he would fight Muhammad Ali for $5M. What Don King did not have, was $10M dollars." There is an important lesson in this for all movie producers: everything is a chicken and egg. Don King got his $10M from the President of Zaire.

I heard a similar story while sitting by the pool at the Loews Hotel in Santa Monica for the American Film Market. "An unknown production company owned by an unknown player amongst the Hollywood scene was pre-selling his big movie. He had Chuck Norris on his movie poster," said the agent who witnessed the spectacle. "He hadn't made the movie yet but he had his title, even made a poster with his star on it. Based on that, and Chuck Norris who was big-time bankable, he was asking people to pre-buy the film. It was action – exactly the kind of thing Norris had been very successful in before. This guy got massive interest. Everyone wanted the film. Before he left AFM, he had $8M in pre-purchases which was probably more than he needed to make the movie. And guess what? *That guy never had talked to or met Chuck*

Norris before. He just made this random poster with Chuck's face on it. He hadn't contacted him in the least. But you know what, he made that movie and Chuck Norris was in it."

Producing is juggling chickens and eggs.

More than one producer

The exact job of the producer is certainly "fuzzy." Perhaps that's the best term. I once watched an episode of television and counted 20 people listed in the credits with a producer title. They were either "producer" or "executive producer" or "associate producer" or "assistant producer." When I first looked at these titles, I assumed "executive producer" must be the more important one since it sounded more important but actually the most important one in that list is plain old: "producer." Even though there is no firm guidelines on what "producer" means, the guidelines are, well, firm-er for the role producer as opposed to executive producer or associate producer.

As a (very) general rule, the executive producer title is for people that had something to do with the funding of the film. Often, they supplied or secured the funding. The associate producer title is a fun title handed out for helping in some other way – like helping with marketing or casting or supplying some other valuable service to the film. There is also consulting producer for someone that worked as a consultant on the film. But the most cherished title is that of plain old "producer." As a (very) general rule, there is only one "producer" and that's the person truly responsible for making the film happen and taking it to market.

A Hollywood producer once gave me a succinct description (and although it's not always accurate, it's a good starting point for understanding): "The producer is the person that has secured the intellectual property rights that the film is based on to initiate the filmmaking process," he said. This could be the option on a book or the possession of or option on a script.

However, the producer isn't always the person who initiated the film. The producer could be brought on later, after a dedicated director or writer has kicked off the process. And because this writer or director might want to focus more on writing and directing – and less on all the logistics – they bring in an outside producer to fill that role.

If you are a filmmaker starting out and you subscribe to the single producer idea, you might want to rethink it depending on the producer you find. You need at least three skillsets from the producer. They have a lot of responsibility and the film won't come together unless they can fulfill three roles. There is a chance that a single producer has all three of these skills or they could have two of them, meaning you only need one additional person. If you are the producer, then you can think of it this way: you will need three hats and if you can't do all three things then you won't be making a movie.

Most importantly, you need a funding producer. This is someone who understands how much recoupable and non-recoupable money is needed for given types of projects and how to secure funding. They are often able to bring buyers into the fold while the scripts are still being written to pre-sell at least some of the key territories. Once presales are secured, they will know how to talk to banks for loans, and how to apply for tax credits where you want to film. This brings us to the next producer that you need.

You will need a "boots-on-the-ground" producer that will arrange those pesky details like cameras and crew and filming things. These folks are normally geographically bound because you don't want to carry the massive cost of flying in an entire crew from out of town to film somewhere. If you're filming in Louisiana or Germany or Toronto, you're going to need a producer to work with a production company in Louisiana or Germany or Toronto. In many of these productions, to maximize your tax credits and government incentives, you want as many people working on the film to be as local as possible. The only people you want to fly in is typically your key talent, which brings us to your final producer.

The talent-oriented producer is last because it's probably the least important although most people mistakenly think it's the most important person. The reality is that if you have the funds, the talent tends to be much more available. Without the funds secured, few producers can get an important actor or actress to read a script and respond (let alone say "yes"). The funding producer should be able to write pay or play offers in such a way that you can get actors to say "yes" or "no." That said, it is helpful to have someone like a casting director or an associate producer with a direct line of communication to the key talent you want to reach.

These three areas need to be juggled at the same time. You want your funding to come into focus as you zero in on a shortlist of key talent for the important roles. Most of these funds are going to be committed, yet contingent on talent. And at the same time, you want a boots-on-the-ground producer to give you a good idea of when the film can be shot, where and for how much – pending final funding and talent availability. Pay or play offers normally come with an idea of timeframe so you will want to know when the film can be shot.

Be wary of producers that have a single set of tools for your project. And if you are a producer or aspire to one, be wary of following any one formula for bringing the film together. Producers, turns out, tend to have a certain way of producing films. They have a network of colleagues to make things happen. They have a repertoire of skills, a methodology and a plan that they normally duplicate no matter the film. When you have a hammer, everything looks like a nail. And likewise, to a producer that successfully raised funds in a particular way, once or twice. Perhaps they made a movie with a particular set of contacts using a particular set of methods. It's likely that they feel that all movies should be made that way. If those methods don't fit your needs, then you will likely need a different producer.

Money first or cast first?

I spoke with a large number of producers about their preferred methods of getting a film made. One of the most popular processes is to get a "letter of intent" from a star to play a role in your film. Once you have that, then go ask for money. The logic being: no one is going to offer to invest in a project that doesn't have talent in the cast. This is what I call the cast-first approach. This is often seen as the safer, slower, steadier path. Certainly, it entails less risk to the producer's personal reputation. Also, it's probably less effective. Reaching out to big name stars without money in hand just to gauge general interest in a project sounds like a big waste of time and mostly it is. Don't get me wrong: if it works for a producer and they can repeat for your project, then you can't argue with what works.

But it's important to note, psychologically, why a producer likes this approach. They send out a few feelers, a few notes to various agents or well-known actors, and wait. It's a great time-management tool. They don't have to invest too much into a project until someone *else* does first. They don't have to put a lot of time, energy and personal reputation into a project *until* they have a big name interested. That's got to be very appealing from a producer's standpoint. "Hey I can't do anything here until I get XYZ person on board." Then everything is easier. So, great. No time invested until things get easier. Who wouldn't want to use a process like this if they could?

Go back to the availability heuristic. Everyone has a story of a star expressing interest in a script and then boom, everything comes together because George Clooney was attached. The problem with all these success stories is that for every one you hear, you also hear 100 more that are still "in process." Sometimes these attempts to get a big-name cast in a role go on for *years* (literally), until the producer tells you that they are giving up on X actor and moving on to Y actor. Rinse, repeat, wait another 18 months.

Given how many projects I hear about winding their way through the cast-first process, I expected it to be the dominant method for getting a project to go forward. But from interviewing producers that have actually made films, I don't think this is true. Just because so many films are *stuck* in this position, doesn't mean it's the best approach or the most popular way of getting something done. After all, if it worked then all those projects wouldn't be stuck in that stage, they'd be done by now. The producers that I talked to usually used a different approach. The other method that was common: get money first. Then when money is in hand, go make offers to cast. Money-first method.

"But I don't understand," I asked the producer. "Isn't the money totally dependent on cast? I mean, you'll get $1M if one actor is in your film but you'll only get $500K if someone less famous is on your film, right?"

"Oh it's almost always conditional funding in one way or another," was the reply. "The investors are usually making an investment based on a list of possible cast and if you don't get that cast or if you get lesser cast then the financial commitment is going to go down. But you get the financial commitment first. And when you have real money committed, you can get all kinds of cast." These producers go after funding with a hypothetical list of cast rather than go after big-name actors with no money. Whether or not you have the money first, you will eventually need to get talent attached to the project. I got some great input on the best approaches to getting those attachments.

Producing and attachments

There are ways of getting someone "important" attached to your film that work better than the typical begging someone to "read my script for free" method. You can send a written offer of money with the script. If the script comes with any money attached, even $1, then the manager and agent of the talent must forward the offer to the actor. They don't have a choice. It doesn't mean the actor will read it but the agent cannot just throw your script away at that point.

You can use a conditional pay or play offer with a more specific timeline (that you got from a production company). The offer could have a specific location and a specific timeline. This makes your film more real even though, in truth, it's not real yet. In that case, you have a financial offer that is contingent on securing the rest of the funding.

You can go to buyers with a contract that says: "Give us $100K in pre-buy commitments for our Nick Nolte movie and if Nolte isn't in the movie, then you owe us nothing." That's a contract you might get signed. Then you get Nick Nolte's signature on a piece of paper that says he'll do your movie for $100K. And, boom, you have a movie. And you don't even have to call the President of Zaire.

22 Financials

What was that budget again?

One of the complications in turning a profit has always simply been understanding the accounting of film, which has normally been quite opaque. I spoke with a Dutch film collections company – who are often contracted to receive and divvy up the films' revenues in adherence to the contracts in place. This service is sort of like putting your film revenues in escrow. Using a collections company is certain to be too expensive for a small indie. But my conversation with the collection executive was enlightening about film accounting.

I asked him how many films break even and he explained how loaded of a question that was. After some thought, his final answer was: "I think from looking at our spreadsheets of many hundreds of films … most films make about 50% of their budgets."

What? Surely, he had misspoken. "You mean, their budgets were 50% of their revenues?" No. I had heard right the first time. Of the films he has worked with – maybe thousands – on average make half their budget back in terms of total revenues.

"That doesn't sound like film is a very good business then." I said.

He chuckled, "Well, you know, budget doesn't mean they spent that money." And, in fact, the devil *was* in the details. The budget, he explained, was a phantom figure that included a lot of non-recoupable money, grants, tax credits, etc. It also included a large amount of deferred compensation which was not ever paid and probably wouldn't ever be paid. A producer could list all sorts of expenses into the budget under the heading of "deferred expenses" which won't get repaid unless the film does amazingly well. These phantom expenses are what make a film (that's a massive hit) show a loss on the bottom line.

"On average, if I had to guess, a film's real out-of-pocket costs are perhaps 30–40% of the budget. So, I would guess, most of the films we work with are profitable even though they only recoup 50% of the so-called budget."

The importance of being on budget

There are numerous anecdotes of well-known producers going above and beyond to stick to budgets.

Directors that started making films with no money like Jason Blum, Robert Rodriguez, Mark Duplass and Ed Burns often talk about how the lack of money forced them to be more creative. When you have larger budgets, goes the thinking, and you are confronted with a filming problem, your mind goes directly to buying something. Buy some toys, a camera or piece of equipment that will solve the problem. And solve it in some ideal, preconceived way. The director with money can get focused on spending money to make that vision a reality.

With no money, your mind goes back to the audience and the story-telling. You can then think through a way to communicate the story to the audience with the tools that you know you have. Instead of spending your mental energy looking for expensive toys, you spend time thinking about your audience. Those toys usually don't deliver a satisfying result anyway.

The most important reason to stick to a budget, however, is that it's a critical part of a business plan. We have commented before that movies are often worth a very specific, predictable amount. A smart producer will know how much in foreign sales your film will generate – or has already generated. Therefore, you know how much you have to spend and spending more than that is how you lose money.

I interviewed one high-wealth individual that funded a film. A relative of his was the director. I could sense immediately how a smart investor would be attracted to the film. This gentleman, having made a fortune in real estate, was indeed quite smart. The film was family entertainment with high dollar possible buyers all over the world. They had a big-name actor in it – i.e. great stunt casting – to sell it. The film generated a staggering $850K in sales. An impressive success story, I thought. Well he didn't think so. The problem? The producers had overspent, driving the total budget over $1.5M. The investor, having invested $1.5M (they did not use the techniques I describe to get non-recoupable funds), suffered a loss of $650K! Blowing your budget will make every other smart thing you do meaningless and will turn what would have been a grand success into a financial fiasco.

Which brings us to …

Financial responsibility and film

A number of producers are no longer referring to investors as "investors." They refer to them as "benefactors" or some synonym. Why? Probably, because they don't want to give the impression they will see the money again. These producers stress the social and artistic value of the movie and inquire what the "benefactor" *really* wants out of the filmmaking process. Translation: It won't be money. In fact, the language used is similar to when you ask someone to donate to a charity. This shift from a movie being an investment to being a charity was disappointing. And must make getting investment much harder.

But I was impressed with the honesty of the approach. I have no moral issue with losing your investor's money if you say: we probably won't make this money back so I hope you're investing for some other reason. It is possible that you have an investor, as one of my producers did, that is wealthy and wants their nephew to get his SAG card. So they pay a production company $225K to make three films ($75K each) each one featuring the nephew. And voila, SAG card. Or you have a "benefactor" that is passionate about the mass death of bees and they want to spend their six-figure bonus to make a documentary on bee death. Okay.

If you have a frank discussion with the investors and have it on good information that the money needed to make this movie is "play money," then good for you. If the investor will forget they wrote the check right after they finish their scotch, then breathe in that freedom. Feel good about those long, luxurious conversations with the creative team about your goals of the film. Go ahead and cross "making money" off the list early in the conversation.

But for the rest of you, I advise that just because you have "new money" (i.e. an investor that's never invested in film before) – often known by its more colorful name: "dumb money" – doesn't mean they don't want their money back.

One veteran director of dozens of films said: "If you want a career in filmmaking, don't burn people. Including don't lose people's money."

23 Raising money the traditional way – beg

There are multiple books and articles out there about how funding for a feature film has been typically put together in the past. They will show you how to put together a film business plan, a pitch deck, a face-to-face pitch, etc. Most of these approaches rely on a few key aspects that I'll outline here. The high-wealth individual and the letter of intent. We have touched on these topics already but let's quickly review. Then we'll rework the model in ways that make the investment better. This will also make it more likely the investor won't lose their shirt. Which, clearly, makes it more likely that you get an investor at all (and another one for your second film).

The high-wealth individual and the UFO

The theory goes like this: find one high-wealth individual (HWI) who is "connecting" with your material. It could be a documentary about a cause close to their heart. Your film could be a narrative but have some social relevance that is important to your HWI. Your HWI perhaps has a bucket list item to make a movie. OK. They want to walk the red carpet (once) or they want to be on Netflix as an executive producer (once). Find a dentist, a surgeon, an uncle, a cousin with an inheritance – someone whose dream it is to invest in a movie. There's a saying about a fool and their money.

So many of these HWI stories get told in filmmaker circles that after some time, I learned the key follow-up question: "Tell me about the *second* movie they invested in?" The answer is always the same: "They never invested in another movie." As Peter from the Cucalorus Film Festival tells us: "You can never use the same investor twice. It's a continual process of burning through investors."

In reality, these HWIs are very, very difficult to find. It's like they are UFOs. A lot of people have seen them but when you look, you can never really find one. However, my search for the Loch Ness monster did turn one up. And as you might guess, the story didn't end well. It was the real estate gentleman who invested in the family film. Even though the film was well designed, executed and sold – the budget overruns meant that our real estate investor lost over $650K. He was none too pleased over the perceived lack of care the producers gave to his funds and he nearly sued. This is often the way these stories end, actually. New money investors, or first time investors, are the most prone to suing precisely because they understand the process less, defer too much to others and lack the expertise to participate in the decisions. Therefore, they are more likely to blame others when things don't go as planned.

Finding an HWI that is willing to take a major risk because they are "connecting with" your material is normally key to getting funding for your project. Another favorite technique is begging your way to having "someone important" read your script and write you a letter of intent to be in your movie.

The letter of intent

This model is begging for someone "important" to read your script. A celebrity or big-name actor to play the lead is normally the way folks go with attachments. Get a celebrity or big-name actor to read the script and express written – yet non-binding – interest in playing a key role in the movie. These commitments are vague in money, vague in time and non-binding on both sides. Producers often love them since emailing scripts is easy and then they don't have to do too much until they get an answer – which they might never get.

This is certainly one approach. And like I've often said, if it works, great. You can't argue with what works. If you can get access to important people and get them to express interest in some concrete way, then you have a good first step. The problem is that this approach doesn't work very often and it takes a considerable amount of time. Waiting on an important person to read a script that is unfunded, for a role that has no money attached and no timeline is the height of vagueness. And is unlikely to motivate even a B-level actor.

You need to get more substance behind your project than just a "please can you read my script?"

24 Before you start begging

Meet your business partners

Earlier, I mentioned that a good sales agent can be a filmmaker's best business partner. But most filmmakers don't utilize a sales agent in the right way. Now I'll explain what I meant and discuss the best ways to work with an agent.

If you haven't engaged with a sales agent nor a distribution firm before making your film, you're already at such a disadvantage that your fortunes are largely now left to chance: Did you make the right movie? Did you put in it the right elements? Does it have the right production value and did you spend the right amount of money? Could you have gotten an aging TV star in your film that would have cost you $10K but would have guaranteed $100K in extra foreign sales? All these questions are better asked at the script-level rather than when the film is in post-production. Again, the notion of "just make a film" without considering all the very real repercussions of various decisions is not good film business regardless if it makes a good film or not.

The key question is: when to engage with a sales agent or distributor? The answer is: much earlier than you think. In fact, the time to establish communication with sales and distribution is during the financing stage while the concept is still in development. Roger Corman, as described above, was selling his films in the presales market before there was even a script. Sales agents that I spoke with varied their answers when asked when was the best time to engage an agent but none went past the point of having a script. In other words, every single agent that I spoke with said that by the time you have a script, you should be engaged with a sales agent. Most of them said that you should be talking to an agent well before you have a script finished. You should be asking them: "Should I make this movie?" and if the answer is positive, then ask more questions.

"How much can I expect from foreign or domestic sales and what needs to happen before we do presales?"

Pre-selling

A presale or negative pickup is when a buyer, working for a distributor, wishes to buy the rights to your film before it's finished. They haven't seen the final product but they've seen a cast list, poster, pitch deck and they probably know the production company or director involved and trust them. It's possible the film is already in production and you can show stills from the set or dailies. If your film is in production, this would lower the risk to the buyer and drive confidence in the final product. Most often, in pre-buys, no money actually changes hands. A contract is drawn up for the specified sales price. Even though this isn't real money, this contract can be taken to a bank or private equity firm who will finance the film based on the amount on the contract (and who signed it). Often these amounts are discounted or loan interest levels are raised based on the strength of the territory involved or the buying entity. If it's a trustworthy buyer who wrote you a presale contract, the interest rate is low and the amount is only discounted slightly. If the territory is unreliable then you might not get the financing at all.

Presales are the ideal way to finance a feature, but how do you get them?

An interesting comment was made by a producer I talked to that makes multiple movies per year, each one pre-sold to multiple foreign territories prior to the first day of shooting. One year it was shark movies. As of the writing of this book, Christmas movies are the new shark movies. Everyone wants one. Sales agents had stressed that filmmakers should partner with an agent by the time a script was finished. But this producer said that this might be too late and disclosing that you already had the script might work *against* you in presales:

> You want the buyer to feel like they have input into the movie they are investing in. That means you don't want to come off like the idea is set in stone. I think part of what they are buying when they pre-buy is the ability to influence the final product. That's why they would pre-buy instead of paying for a movie that's already done. This way they can tell the filmmakers to customize the ending or beginning or the level of violence or action or whatever. In some ways, it's better to come to them with a general idea or an outline and not a full script.

What you need from your sales agent is a list of recommended cast. Who will make this film worth $1M? Which stars do you need to sell the film in Europe, China, Asia, etc? Ask them for a list of five to ten stars that you can realistically get for the budget you are working with and will result in the film being more sellable.

As part of the financing process, the experienced producers said mostly the same thing: "Presell first. You don't have to presell every territory and you shouldn't, especially if you think you'll have a good film. But sell at least one major territory like Germany, England, or Australia. Securing 20%+ of your budget in presales is important for a few big reasons." Why?

First, committing to pre-selling a few territories forces you to get real about the prospects of your film before you start spending real money. If sales agents and distributors continually tell you "no" to any possibility of presales then you should re-work your project or get a new one.

Second, by selling multiple territories or having at least one major territory already sold, this draws the buyers from all other territories into negotiations and bids up the price later on. Once you have a film that has been sold at least a few times already, everyone wants to talk to you at least to have a look.

Third, securing presales gives you a strong hand to find your next big source of funding, bank loans, described later on.

Last, cash flow. Roger Corman used presales to fund his films. From his perspective, as a production company, if he had to raise money then wait for the film to generate revenues in order to pay off investors then he had a cash flow problem. He couldn't make that many movies since it takes so much time for a movie to finish production, post-production, get released and then generate revenues. If he's dependent on those revenues coming in to make his next picture then he's waiting a long time. From a business perspective, if he pre-sold his films, then he'd have a much stronger cash flow. He could then use the presales money to immediately make another film – therefore assuring not only would he not lose money but he could make many more films. Good business.

Presales tips

Engaging with sales agents and even better, a distributor, at the earliest possible stage is best. Even if you just have a treatment, synopsis, poster, logline or a pitch deck. Log onto IMDB and Cinando and research similar films with similar budget ranges that you are looking for. Find foreign and domestic distribution companies who buy them. Start the engagement process as early as possible.

One distribution company that I talked to still regularly does presales – they refer to them as "negative pickups" – i.e. picking up a title prior to it being available in the market. They discussed the frequency at which this is done and the advantages to the buyer: namely the financial advantage. When a buyer picks up a film prior to it being finished, the buyer only spends 75–80% or less of what it expects the film to be worth once finished.

Negative pickups or pre-buys are good business for the buyer, not only for reasons of financial savings, but the buyer normally doesn't need to exchange any real cash. Often times, no money changes hands although sometimes a deposit can be negotiated. The distributor explained:

> Even though no money might be changing hands, there's still some risk for us (i.e. the buyer). Because we are buying a film to fill a slot that's down the line and if that film doesn't materialize or isn't of the quality that we expect then that slot might go unfilled or we might have to overspend at the last minute to fill it. And regardless, if we make that deal with one group then it's a deal that could have gone to some other team.

And how best to introduce yourself to these buyers – as a filmmaker or producer? At first the distributor in question was quite open: "We are making deals like this all the time. All throughout the year. Filmmakers can literally just email or call us or meet us at a Film Festival like AFM." But then he gets more guarded. Hey, it's not *that* easy. "Well, you need some credibility that you can deliver. I would suggest aligning yourself with someone we've worked with before. Either find a producer that's worked with us successfully in the past, or an executive producer or investor."

Find producers, executive producers, associate producers associated with movies similar to yours that sold to buyers you're interested in. They can be found on Cinando, IMDBPro and other online sources.

Whether you're working directly with distributors or you are working with a sales agent that is representing your (not yet made) movie, the process is the same. Get the idea in front of buyers and agents and get as much feedback as you can. If you are hearing the same negative answers then you will need to rework the concept to be more viable in the marketplace. But the time to rework your concept to be more profitable is now, before shooting begins. The time to hear that your film has no buyers and is essentially worthless is not after it's already done.

If the concept is viable, agents and distributors can also help you in the fund-raising for the film. Many distribution channels like Hallmark, Lifetime, Showtime and Netflix are now completely funding and owning the films. Sales agents often have a production arm to their firm where they finance films they know they can sell. If none of these fish are biting, you probably don't have good bait.

Although many experienced producers explained they pre-sell everything first, they had the advantage of great track records and long term relationships. Other producers I spoke with were more negative about presales. They would say the presales markets were no longer viable unless you "had Keanu Reeves in your movie." Or they would say the offers currently out there for presales were no longer even worth it. Just $5K here and there wasn't enough to fund a feature film.

Their feelings were that features now had to be finished to attract buyers. There were just too many films out there, they would say. So let's discuss what these producers (who were more negative about the presales market) were saying. These were successful producers so they have developed alternative methods to not lose money. They might not have enough presales to fully fund a film (which would essentially eliminate the financial risk) but they have methods to reduce the risk dramatically to the investor.

25 Reducing the risk when presales don't work

Many producers are still using presales to great effect. But some will tell you that presales is a game you can play only when you have friends in high places. What if you find yourself circling around looking for a chicken to make the egg then an egg to hatch the chicken only to repeat?

There are things you can do to get your project moving and reduce the risk to the investor: maximize non-recoupable funds. Get assurances from buyers just short of pre-buy. Use development money.

Maximize non-recoupable money

Non-recoupable funds are funds provided to your film that the funding party is not expecting back. The best example of this, we've already gone over: revenues from presales. There is also grants and tax incentives. All these funds are put together to pay for the making of the film and the providers do not need to be paid back. A large number of films are made with majority non-recoupable funds.

It is your objective as filmmaker and/or producer to reduce the recoupable money needed to make the film – otherwise known as equity investment. You must increase non-recoupable money. Recoupable money, or equity, is money you need to raise and it's at-risk. Even if you can't eliminate equity investment completely, often you can reduce it dramatically which has the advantage of being able to sell 100% of a film for some small percentage of the budget. If I could get 50% stake in a $500K movie for only $100K, then that's a more attractive investment than having to spend $250K for the same result. It also means that if that $500K movie only nets $200K in revenues, then it still breaks even. Because you still return 100% of the equity investor's money back to them despite showing a large loss on the profit and loss sheet.

Normally, this will mean filming in a tax-advantaged location. You will need to work with a "boots-on-the-ground" producer and a production company in a state or a country with large tax incentives. This is increasingly a *must* in filmmaking. Many states only allow "tax credits" (as opposed to rebates) which are only convertible to cash if you actually have a large tax liability to that state or country. However, in most cases, the tax credits are "transferable" which means they can be sold. Not 100% of the value of those credits but perhaps 90% can be converted to cash. For smart producers, this is just too much money to ignore. 30% is a typical tax credit and even for a film with a comparably small budget of $300K: that's $90K – a huge dollar figure. Check online for a list of states and countries with the most attractive tax incentives.

Short of a pre-buy

Getting a contract to pre-buy your film from a distributor is not the only way a distributor can help you reduce the financial risk. Some distribution firms might not commit to a contracted, financial minimum guarantee but they will commit to distribute your film in that territory. If the distributor has a long track record and is a coveted channel in that territory, then that might be a significant win. If that firm gives you sales estimates (i.e. what they think you will make when the film is finished) and that firm has a reputation of supplying accurate sales figures, then this will give your investor some level of confidence.

When you meet with distributors, you can ask all the pointed questions. How many movies like this do they buy? What quality and budget levels? What are some examples of films they have bought, similar to your idea, in the past? How did those movies do in their region and what is their willingness to buy more movies like this? If you get a lot of distributors telling you that you have a great idea, then investment becomes easier. A pre-buy agreement is the most powerful. Sales estimates specific to a territory from a given distributor who has a long track record in that territory is second. Sales estimates from a sales agent are the least reliable.

Use development financing

Development financing is when a small percentage of the budget is raised in order to form a film LLC/corporation. The money can be used to retain a casting director and a line producer so that a professional budget can be drafted and offers to key talent can be sent. These funds help give the impression to external parties that the film project is "real." And substantially increases the odds of it materializing. It might not, by itself, raise the odds that the film is a good idea but it certainly is a small sum that dramatically increases the chances the film is made at all.

26 Press – the gift that keeps on giving

With review aggregators gaining in popularity, the press you gain for your film can persist, easily accessible on the internet for years or decades. It's a permanent record of the quality of your work. It carries the weight of unbiased, expert opinion and, if you have more than ten reviews that more or less agree with each other, social proof that validates your film. Buyers and consumers will check your press before deciding to spend money on your movie.

Five big reasons why you need to get press for your film:

1. It will help you with a distribution deal. Get press earlier than you think. Normally, people think of press when the film is released in the US. That's a great time to get press. But these days, just getting any US release (at least one with money attached, like a minimum guarantee) is so hard that you need to consider getting press before you sign a distribution deal in order to boost your chances of getting a good one. Even if the film hasn't been shown yet, get interviews or articles about the making of the film.

2. It will help you get into difficult festivals. Once you are in festivals, the festival gives you another opportunity to push for more media coverage as well.

3. It will help your future as a filmmaker. Anyone looking to work with you in the future will look up your projects online and glance through the press you got. You must think beyond this film. The press clippings and critic quotes are things you can use for your next pitch.

4. It represents expert opinion that validates your film which is the most powerful form of advertising. If you run a social media campaign, you will need to point your fans to your positive press, not just your trailer. If you have good reviews, you will photoshop

quotes into your poster. If you have a good rotten tomatoes score, you should edit it into your trailer.

5.   Most obviously, it will connect your film's audience to the release when the film goes out to the region.

Making press happen

Press and publicity is one of the most problematic areas for independent filmmakers. Trying to do-it-yourself – i.e. finding journalists, then emailing or calling them – is usually a disaster. Like I discussed in the obstacles of film journalism back in Part 2, most journalists not only won't but really just can't cover your film. If it's not playing in Boston for five days then it's a waste of time trying to corner the film critic from the Boston Globe at Sundance. They can't write about your film even if they wanted to. Ditto for almost every journalist that you've ever heard of, because unless it's playing in theaters in their city, they are policy-bound to leave you out.

Likewise, most publicity firms will start at $5–10K monthly to support your film with a minimum of three months. The results you can hope for would be typically a few articles or reviews published when they are done. Managed-DIY distributors won't publicize your film. The best you can hope for would be if they facilitate an introduction to a firm that will – thus the "managed" terminology. But they probably won't offer you many options except perhaps sending you a "guide to promoting your film through social media." Professionally, I've been trying to crack this nut myself. Check out the latest news from Bunker 15 Films (www.bunker15films.com) to see what is the most up to date info on getting indie films noticed on Rotten Tomatoes or other film aggregators. Reach out to me and I'll keep you apprised of the latest research in this area but one thing is clear: you need to get press for your film!!

DIY your press

The best process to DIY your press is fairly straight-forward. It's a slog that's labor- and time-intensive but it's possible. Research Rotten Tomatoes and start pulling down movie after movie that are similar to the one you're making and find the critics who reviewed them.

The critical issue is this: it must have the same kind of distribution! If you have a film (that you feel) is like *Lady Bird*, don't think the critics that reviewed *Lady Bird* will take an interest in your film. That is, unless you can match *Lady Bird*'s distribution (i.e. standing ovation at the Toronto Film Festival and 1,200 screens around the country).

If you have an iTunes film, find films on Rotten Tomatoes that were iTunes (only) movies. Create a long list of critics that reviewed multiple iTunes films. You will need a very long list, perhaps 200. Once you have this list, you can start to research their contact information. Let's assume you can find a decent email address for 35% of them. Thus, you have 70 contacts. Put your best pitch together in email and fire off 70 emails to these critics roughly 6–8 weeks before your film is released online. Let's assume you hear back from ten of them. One out of seven is a fairly good percentage so I'm assuming you have a really good pitch. Send those ten critics a screener link (i.e. an online URL to the video of your film so they can watch via Vimeo or some other movie hosting site), a link to your movie stills (most critics will want to post a movie still with their review, *not* your movie poster) and press package. Then pray that five of them review your film. You will also need to remind them multiple times, as nicely as possible.

Brace yourself for some negativity. Journalists are not known for their gentile tact. You will get some snotty replies, flat rejections, and there is normally at least a few that will accuse you of some sort of ethical or moral violation for trying to promote your own film. I assure you these folks are just having a bad day. There is nothing inherently wrong or nefarious in trying to promote your own film. Some newspapers might have rules where a journalist cannot talk directly with a filmmaker or producer but there's nothing wrong with asking.

Social media will not save you

Currently, there is tremendous hype around paid social media campaigns. Facebook made $55B in 2018 while Google AdWords continues a precipitous ascent in revenues as well. Whenever there is tremendous hype around a product it is, without doubt, over-priced. In 2019, you will have a hard time structuring a Google AdWords campaign without paying a few dollars per click. Facebook ads (which are normally charging you just to display the ad instead of how many clicks you are getting), according to research, are costing at least $5 simply to show the ad to 1,000 people. If you can swing a 1% click-through-rate, then that's ten clicks and you're paying 50 cents per click. That's very generous but let's assume you manage to pay just 50 cents per click. Let's run the numbers.

Say you're trying to get your audience to pay for a streaming view of your movie that costs $4.99 on Amazon Video. Of this, Amazon will keep half, your distributor keeps another 30%, leaving the film producers with approximately $1.75 each time someone rents their film online. Let's say your paying just 50 cents *per click*! Then you're hoping that one out of every three clicks will lead to a purchase. But if that's what you're hoping, then you don't know anything about click-through conversion rates, because they are not even close to one out of three.

If you do choose to make a modest investment in social media to spread the word in some way, perhaps hoping that something catches the zeitgeist or the attention of the masses – then you must again, go back to press. You shouldn't be advertising just your trailer and your poster. You need to be advertising your film's positive press. It validates the film with social proof and expert opinion. You should have critic quotes on your poster. You should have your Rotten Tomatoes score digitally inserted into your trailer. Even if your ads work, a consumer will not go directly to rent your film. They will go to a review aggregator to read reviews. Make sure some reviews are there to read.

Buyers read reviews

Recall the message: "Foreign and domestic buyers might not be watching your film before they decide to buy it." Netflix, Hulu, HBO or that large Chinese buyer might not see your film before stroking a check, but they will have checked a review aggregator. If there is no score then they know the film didn't get much traction and might move on to a film that's gotten more recognition. However, if a respectable number of critics gave the film solid marks, your odds of making your investment back sky rocket.

Conclusion

There's a well-known book about Buddhism called *If you meet the Buddha on the road, kill him*! The message isn't (I hope) so much about homicide, it's that if anyone is telling you that they know the absolute answers then they are lying. The same goes for making movies. You know they are lying because there are no answers. There may be answers for you or answers from your point of view. But there are no universal answers that are right for everyone, all the time.

The methods that take you to a successful career in filmmaking depend on your skills, resources, experience and personal network. Each person is in a unique position with a unique perspective and goals that are all their own. This book is a collection of the best advice from the business side of the filmmaking industry. Whether you follow these directions exactly or not, you are far better off hearing their stories than having to learn these lessons the hard way. Knowing the terrain allows you to find your own way. Or, if you're so inclined, it allows you to use a well-worn path that others have tread.

My journey from tech entrepreneur into the film industry has been a blast. Having spent the better part of two years researching how to make movies without losing money, I know I have moved into a great industry. For all its turmoil, entertainment is thrilling, creatively challenging and ripe with opportunity. This is the time to be in entertainment.

But you already know that. That's why you're reading. It's a great time in film. It might not seem like it all the time. Industries are cyclical. There are ebbs and flows. Ebbs are actually when you want to get into something. Business models that are now in flux will stabilize. It will become easier to monetize small films in the years to come. Demand will continue to rise.

After spending much of the last two years researching films and finance, I know now there are ways of making movies with a responsible, repeatable strategy that doesn't entail finding new money each time.

I hope I've opened the door, saved you two years and let you in on some secrets previously known only to the experienced insiders. Whether you take one of the paths outlined in the book or if you make your own path using these lessons, you're better armed to make a successful career.

Technology will change but telling stories in a compelling way will always be the key. The world needs storytellers. The world will always need the artist. Making a work of art that people love and people want to see isn't compromising your art – it's elevating it.

Top ten lessons

Although there are a myriad of lessons, tips and techniques throughout the book, I will conclude with some of my favorites.

#1 – Let art embrace commerce

Commercial is not the opposite of good. Don't internalize belief systems that undermine your career. Even the best filmmakers think hard about making their films enjoyable, accessible and they care deeply if people come to see them. All the elements that make a film good can make it watchable and enjoyable. You can make a good film about even the most commercial ideas. Making a children's film about "holiday magic" can just as easily become your tour de force that is appreciated for generations. There is no law saying that a commercial success needs to be empty of artistic value.

The artist must make peace with the market. Commerce and artistic expression should not be adversaries. In fact, artistic excellence and wide audience appeal can make powerful allies. The art film that is a hit at the box office is likely to see the highest honors at the Oscars and Golden Globes. The director that can marry financial success and cinematic excellence is likely to get the top actors in Hollywood calling them rather than the other way around. Making a movie that is crowd-pleasing and critic-pleasing is the highest form of the art. Inserting crowd-pleasing aspects into the quality film elevates it rather than denigrates it. Likewise, inserting meaning and substance into crowd-pleasing entertainment, in turn, elevates it as well.

#2 – Festivals are the vehicle, not the destination

Don't get drawn in exclusively to the festival circuit without understanding how it will work for your career and if it will benefit the value of your film. Don't let the availability heuristic fool you into thinking just because festivals are everywhere and you always know who won the recent big ones that that is the definition of success.

Thinking of festivals as the vehicle and not the destination is the key. Research the festivals that your buyers will be at first. Create a short-list of festivals based on what will have value to your film. Find publicity teams that can introduce you to the programming people at the festivals that will have the most impact for you. Reach out to buyers before the festivals and invite them to the screenings. Promote your film's profile well before the festival. Dan Myrick of *The Blair Witch Project* noted that well before it opened at Sundance, the movie had huge buzz and a great social media following already. And don't make your film try to fit into a stereotype of a typical "festival film" – I don't think Myrick would have made *The Blair Witch Project* if he was thinking like that.

#3 – Who is your buyer?

Understand that your buyer (i.e. the distribution channel who will buy the rights to your film) might be different than your audience (i.e. the consumer and viewer) and you will need to juggle both ideas. Like Pixar when they make one scene that has to entertain on two levels, that is now you. That means continuously shaping and reshaping your themes and ideas to fit them better. Do you want your backup buyers to be televisions stations and if so, what does that mean for the genre, structure and elements of your film?

Pay close attention to how the film is sold to audiences and buyers. A lesser director might not pay as much attention to superficial aspects of their film like the poster, trailer or press quotes but this is what buyers use to decide whether to buy your film. It's more than superficial. They enjoy the steak but they buy the sizzle.

#4 – Lower your budget!

This is a rare bit of advice that you will see here *and* from Mark Duplass, Robert Rodriguez and so many big-name filmmakers that started from nothing. The key advantage you have as a producer or filmmaker is that people have no idea how much production value you can bring to the table with a tiny budget. Technology can now make your $250K ultra-low budget film look like it has a budget of $2.5M. Cameras are good enough to film without lighting equipment. Gareth Edwards said post-production digital editing allowed him to film more easily in public places. Before, he couldn't because of the plethora of copyrighted images always popping up in the background. Posters of the latest Manchester United games and McDonalds arches can now be easily edited out in post-production. Digital explosions can be purchased for a nominal cost and edited into your scene of actors jumping out of windows, thereby eliminating the need for actually dangerous explosions on set.

Technology is way ahead of what your buyers understands. Make your $2.5M film for $200K, hire a name actor for $50K and you're in business.

Budgets also need to come down because revenues have come down. Don't use 15 year old budgets when revenues are not what they were 15 years ago. If you can make 2004 money then use a 2004 budget. When revenues are being cut by two-thirds, your budgets need to follow suit. And with technology now, you can.

#5 – Network with business people who have access to resources

You must understand the business side of your art. All artists live in the real world and must make a living. If you truly understand how the financial side of your industry works, and surround yourself with good entertainment lawyers and representatives then you put yourself in a position to survive on just your art. This gives you the freedom to create things that please yourself as well as others – both critically and commercially.

Establish working relationships early with those professionals in the supply and distribution chain. Meet sales agents, distribution firms, end-buyers of films and film lawyers so you can map out the lifecycle of your film before it's even in final script stage. Before you have a script, you should be talking the idea over with agents and distributors. Occasionally, you should come up from the script or step away from the camera. Widen your view of the film industry. The film industry contains legions of people that work to monetize a film after it's already done. You need to know them.

#6 – Stunt cast

Real estate is location, location, location. Movies are cast, cast, cast. If Francis Ford Coppola (with two Oscars on his shelf) isn't too good for stunt casting Marlon Brandon into *Apocalypse Now*, neither are you.

Using pay-or-play offers or holding fees will almost certainly force the agent or manager to forward the script to the actor. They won't be able to just throw it away without showing it to the actor. Give the actor a chance to do something different – something, hopefully, they would like to do to grow in their craft. You won't be able to offer studio-money so you need to offer something they want to do. And think through carefully how you will use the actor once they get to set because they won't be there for many days. Film as many scenes as possible and make sure they are scattered throughout the film, the beginning, middle and end. It's a process to get them and it's a process to utilize the actor in the right way but it adds value to the film and that's what matters.

#7 – Make sure your producer thinks money first, cast second

Your producer will need to do three very difficult things. First, they need to be able to logistically make the film happen, bringing crew and cameras to set. Second, they need to be able to reach and get agreement from talent that will bring value to the production. Third, and most important, they need to secure the funding – which is, more and more, the most complicated and important part of the process. You might need to engage with more than one producer. Find producers, executive producers or associate producers with complementary skills. Don't be afraid to move on if their methods don't fit your project.

There's nothing wrong with a cast-first approach if it comes together quickly, but casting is easier with funds committed. Most of the smart producers now are getting some kind of funding and that is what opens the doors to talent.

#8 – Bring something unique to the table

There are many ways you can bring something of unique value to the table. You can shoot an outstanding short film to show someone what your film will look like when it's fully funded. You can get a kickstarter or indiegogo campaign fully funded to prove out the viability of your audience. You could start an Instagram account and get 100,000 followers or get an option on the rights to a book you love. Do you have a script that has won awards? A relationship with a director or an actor?

#9 – Understand the importance of press

There are professionals out there that you can partner with that make sure indie films get the press they need to complete their journey to the market. It's impossible to build a career as a filmmaker if your film is met with deafening silence from the great, big world of film journalism.

Even a handful of critics praising and triggering interest in your film can mean the world to a filmmaker trying to kickstart their career.

#10 – And last ... go make something

Finally, when you have done all this and have all this working for you, follow the advice of Ava DuVernay, Mark Duplass and countless other creative experts, and stop asking for advice. Just go make a short or a movie – make something! Don't even talk to me. Stop procrastinating. Go make a movie. Then get back to me.

And when I say "get back to me," I mean it. I would love to hear about your successes as well as your hard-earned lessons learned (i.e. failures). Tell me what's working for you and what's not. There is no one right answer. Go out, make a plan for success, execute and tell me how it went. You can be a case study in the next edition! I have recently been particularly involved in the area of film publicity. It is so critical to monetizing independent film. Go to my website at www.bunker15films. com to contact me, see the latest best practices on how to make a splash with your indie and, of course, good ways of making films that don't lose money!

Appendix

Case studies, interviews and producer profiles

Case study

Micro-budget filmmaking – Marcus Mizelle

Introduction

Marcus has made three feature films – *Half Empty* (2009), *Actor for Hire* (2015) and *Chameleon* (2019) – each would qualify as micro-budget. In his examples, he's using an approach similar to Ed Burn's *Independent Ed* where most of the talent and crew are working for free. But even in this approach, we see from his case studies that you still need a significant amount of investment to get your film distributed and viewed by the public. Marcus' approach shows one method to get a film produced and sold while using a small enough level of funding that you can make the movie without significant risk to your investor. We have heard again and again from experts that one way to minimize the risk to the investor is by lowering your budgets as low as possible and Marcus gives us a good look into how that can be done.

Pre-conditions

First, let's look at what makes this type of filmmaking possible. Because this approach might not be for you or it might be much harder for you than it was for someone like Marcus. One of the biggest pre-conditions here is that you are currently working as a film industry or crew professional with access to at least some filmmaking equipment. In this scenario, it's best that you work in a filmmaking town. Marcus has lived and made films in industry towns like Wilmington, New Orleans and Los Angeles. Wilmington has, at least when Marcus was living there from 2005–2010, a high concentration of film industry professionals relative to other occupations.

What makes this type of filmmaking even more likely is that the industry in Wilmington tends to be seasonal. This means there are downtimes in many film crews schedules where there is not much to do.

Since this is a small community, many of them know each other and trade favors. "In-kind" services, as they are called. You work on my project and I'll work on your project, etc. Los Angeles also offers opportunities to make something for very little by accessing the endless trove of hungry creatives looking to be a part of a strong project, though this route takes a bit more fishing for your specific needs, compared to a more concentrated community such as Wilmington.

Marcus, without reading *Independent Ed*, has taken a cue from the tips that Ed Burns puts in the book. He filmed his three movies the same way – with crews working mostly for free, in between other, paying gigs. This required writing a flexible script that could be filmed a little here and a little there. No locations have to be camped out in for multiple days. Each of his features were filmed over 2–3 months on the calendar but didn't require nearly that many consecutive days of filming.

He found that one of the keys to success was to *not* execute pre-production on all days of the shoot up-front. Since the shooting would stretch out for so long, it was impossible to predict that far into the future. He found success by doing pre-production a week or two at a time for a two to four day shooting block, then allowing the team to catch their collective breaths before executing another block of pre-production, which involved scheduling the shoot, wrangling props and wardrobe, locking locations, etc. This method was repeated until the film was completed.

Like Tom Malloy, he used standing stages like Silver Dream Factory in Anaheim to film on pre-made sets for rent. The standing stages were one mile outside Los Angeles County, making it easier to film without permits and unions. For *Chameleon*, Marcus also financed the camera on his own dime which provided flexibility while shooting on a non-consecutive schedule, and once photography was completed, sold the camera for nearly the original purchase amount.

Short first

Shooting your concept as a short-film first is a common recommendation. Shorts can be executed much easier for in-kind services – easier to get friends together for a weekend than it would be for, say, three weeks. These shorts can be used to woo an investor to fund the rest of the film. And, if planned well, the short footage can be used as part of the film itself. Thus if the short is 12 minutes long, that's 12 minutes that doesn't need to be re-shot when it's time to make the film. Marcus did this for all three of his features.

Advice to filmmakers

Marcus has several key lessons from his first few features. First, there are hidden film costs that don't come into play until after the production is finished. As I've stressed before, filmmaking still costs real money. Even if you have a film finished and did it all for free, you might get sticker shock when you realize how much it's going to cost to put your baby on iTunes!

"Most first-time filmmakers think pre-production and production will be the bulk of the costs, but that's not usually the case, in my experience. In fact, when you're doing micro-budget filmmaking, it's the post-production expenses such as sound mixing, legal/delivery costs, marketing materials such as artwork/trailer and festival submissions that are the biggest expenses. Because those expenses, often, can only be scaled down so much. Lawyers can only be so cheap and if you need a legal review to obtain E&O Insurance for your film for your distributor or sales agent, that's going to be thousands of dollars right there," says Marcus

In fact, most of his production costs were limited to food and travel expenses for his crew since most of them were working for free. *Half Empty*, the total budget was around $9K – only half of which was production. About $5K for production and the average crew size was anywhere from 10–20 on that production. Recall that his first production was ten years ago and that average crew size would probably be smaller today. The other $5K was for post-production such as music and sound editing/design costs. Other than $2K won at a film festival, the film was not profitable – though the film has been viewed more than 100,000 times since being uploaded online, and the many learning experiences were invaluable.

Actor for Hire had a larger budget of about $60K but only $14K of this was production! *Actor for Hire* didn't do as well financially as his current effort, *Chameleon*, but it did show in 25 film festivals and garnered a ton of press in all the major industry outlets. Marcus applied to over 150 festivals with the film. The total tab for festival applications was over $8K. Although the film didn't do as well financially, each of the actors and talent associated got enough exposure through its large festival showing that they have enjoyed other roles and jobs as a result of the film. The investor – a hometown friend who wanted to work with Marcus after seeing his directing reel – was also able to write off a majority of his loss. Thus, it falls into that category of film that might not have recouped its investment, but it succeeded in other areas. First, the amount it lost was low because the investment was low. Second, the crew, the talent and everyone involved profited from the film's wide festival exposure to advance their careers significantly.

Chameleon is the most recent of Marcus' features, released in 2019. Financed by small deposits over four investors (one being Marcus). It is currently selling in foreign markets now and its success shows that Marcus' approach is improving. The film was done on a budget of only $36K after their initial investor pulled out at the last minute. Despite the financial setback, the production team decided to still make the film with only $7K needed for production! The rough breakdown: $3K for locations, $2K on food and travel, and around $2K on props and miscellaneous rentals. $14K for post-production (which included a big "friends-and-family discount" on sound mixing/designing and color timing the film) as well as marketing elements such as the trailer and artwork – crucial yet often overlooked elements when selling and exhibiting the film; roughly $10K for delivery fees such as E&O Insurance, legal/clearance reports, Continuity Reports, DCPs and Captions; $3K in festival applications; and $2K to hire a publicist to place a single Screen Daily ad for the film prior to the Berlin Film Festival.

Domestic and foreign sales have already been achieved, and with more offers and interest emerging every film market, *Chameleon* is well on its way to making its investment back – so Marcus is improving his approach incrementally as he moves forward. If you can keep expenses low enough and make a marketable film, you can likely make the money back *and* advance the careers of the people involved.

Interview with legendary film school teacher Dov Simens

Dov has been teaching students how to break into the business and make films for 30 years. Quentin Tarantino, Guy Ritchie, Will Smith, Queen Latifah, Matthew Vaughn and hundreds of film festival winners. All attended his acclaimed two-day film course. In our talk, he starts with a familiar refrain we've heard again and again through this book: "It's called show *business*, not show *art*. It's a business and if you focus on making a work of art, you're not likely to go anywhere," he says with his typical no-nonsense approach.

Show business is marketing business

"The other thing to remember is that show business is a marketing business, not a filmmaking business," he says. The studios are mostly in marketing. "It's true that you will need the one thing I can't teach you and I don't think can be taught: talent. But even when you tell a unique story that no one has seen before: when you're done with the film, you're back in the marketing business."

The marketing of your film begins with obfuscating your budget. I raise the issue early in the book that data is hard to come by and accurate data is nearly impossible to come by. Dov reviews one of the key reasons why this is the case.

"Nowhere in the world is it common practice to tell the consumer how much the product cost to manufacture." And he is definitely right. There's no argument. No product in the world puts on the brochure: this product costs $7 to manufacture – so it must be worth your 8 bucks.

Therefore, it's Dov's advice to play like the rest of Hollywood and inflate your perceived budget. If you have a $250K film, you shouldn't feel bad about telling the world it cost "just under $1M." And if your budget was $100K then why not tell the world, the movie was made for: "just under half a million." Welcome to Hollywood, he would say. Exaggerating your budget, like stunt casting and drafting, is something that everybody does – even the biggest names.

"Do you really think *Avatar* actually cost $300M to make? Are you kidding, you could buy a country for that amount. Everybody exaggerates their budgets. It's marketing." Good point.

And knowing you're in the marketing business means chopping off the lion's share of your budget for just that: marketing. "With a $100K film, you will need to use half of it, $50K, for marketing. Make the movie with the other $50K." And he acknowledges that, with legal and delivery costs being over $10K, you're really making the film with $40K or less. For a $250K ultra-low budget film? "You will want to budget $100K for marketing. Festivals, publicists, etc."

The details of low-budget filmmaking

In his course, he breaks down exactly how you make the film for this small budget. He gives the highlights to me. "You just do the math. How much do you have for acting? You'll need $200 per day per actor – so you might only have enough money for three to five actors in your movie. You might have enough for either a 2 weeks shoot with no stunts or special effects. Or, if you have $100K filming budget, you might have enough for an 18-day shoot. With a 90-page script, you will be able to do five pages per day with three takes per scene."

If this is going to be a first film with such a tiny budget, you will almost certainly have to be a single-location film – like *Clerks*, *Rope*, *Saw*, *12 Angry Men*, *Burial*, *Phonebooth*, or any Roger Corman Beach Blanket movie. This is like a stage play on camera, he says. Many successful films were filmed almost entirely in a single location, so don't feel hemmed in.

Dov has his own opinions on cast, however, that give a different take on what I've heard before. "Don't get any TV actors in your movie. Your audience can see these people for free every day on TV. No one wants them in your movie." And he also knows that because of your budget, you won't be getting any movie names either. Dov is also aware of the current dynamics for film finance. He says that with streaming now, you should be able to recoup a $50–70K from a micro-budget film, on a first film. But not more than that.

The job isn't over with the finished film

To his credit, Dov's film school does not do what many film schools and film books do: treat the finished film as the end-all-be-all goal. He advises when the film is finished: spend a large portion of your film's marketing budget on a publicist or a producer's agent that will apply to the top festivals *for you*. "You don't apply, they apply for you," he says. Hopefully, these are the same (high-priced) publicists working with top films getting into Sundance, Telluride, Cannes, Berlin, etc. These publicists are paid well because they ought to know the top programming directors at festivals. There may be 8,000 film festivals in the world but only 10–15 of them have any *acquisition executives* going to them. Those are the only festivals you care about. If buyers aren't going to a festival, then you don't need to either.

Buyers are your key demographic. Launch a social media campaign targeting just 50–100 people – i.e. the key acquisition executives at the studios you want to buy your film. You'll need a campaign that will spin the offers you already have on your movie. You likely will have zero – but your campaign will want to hype it up to make it seem like there are "offers coming in." Welcome to Hollywood, as he would say.

Even with this strategy, there are no guarantees. Your film might go nowhere. In which case, you go back and make another one. A lot of successful people in this business had a slew of flops and failures and false starts before they made something good that got recognized.

But this gives you the best chance to spend only a small amount of money, get it into the top festivals, and get the film in front of top executives.

"Everyone wants to start in the middle – with a $750K budget. To get approved to make a $20M film, you first make a successful $2M film. The way you make a $2M film is by making a successful $200K (or less) film. And, of course, to get the $200K, you might have to make a $20K film with 2 iPhones, three actors driving around in minivans. Don't try to start in the middle, start at the bottom and work your way up." And even with the $20K film, he hammers the same point: "If you make a movie for $20K, it will be $5K for production, $10K for legal and delivery and $5K for marketing."

Dov expresses the same kind of exasperation that led me to do the research in this book. His focus is primarily on what you're going to do with the film once it's done. How are you going to market it? Will you have the money to market it? He also spends a lot of time and energy focusing on how to not waste a lot of money when you make your first film. Limiting the risk and being realistic about your chances of making a half a million dollar investment is important. It's better to make a small, one-location film that gets into a major festival than to find a surgeon willing to give you a half a million dollars which will just be lost on a film that no one will see when it's done.

Dov's live "Two-day Film School" and "Streaming Film School" can be found at WebFilmSchool.com. Welcome to Hollywood.

Case study
Niche moviemaking – Tom Malloy

Introduction

Tom Malloy of Glass House Distribution has been writing, acting in and producing films since the late 1990s. He's raised over $25M in private equity for film production since he started his career. His distribution company, Glass House, was so-named to highlight transparency with the filmmaker as a reaction to so many distribution companies in the market that don't do an adequate job of keeping their filmmakers aware of the expenses and the revenues associated with the selling of their films.

Tom also has a production company, Trick Candle Productions, that selectively produces high quality, market-driven films. Tom has cultivated a long career in film producing by making sure to caretake his investor's money – which means making movies without losing money. There are never guarantees with equity investment, but he's had great success and was happy to share a few of his stories.

Movie: *#Screamers* (2016)

Tom got the idea for *#Screamers* in October of 2015 taking his daughter on a hayride for Halloween. Tom had recently seen *Catfish* where a pair of brothers go on a hunt to discover who their new social media "friend" really was. Tom wondered what *Catfish* would be like if it were horror movie where things took a gruesome turn mid-way through. Of course, *Catfish* did not take such a turn but Tom wondered out loud (i.e. on social media) if people thought it would be a good idea. He was encouraged by the strong social media enthusiasm for a found footage horror movie in the vein of *The Blair Witch Project* and *Paranormal Activity* but with an internet twist. In retrospect, Tom says, found footage might have been overdone at the time. But following in the footsteps of successful films is typically a good approach.

Development

After coming up with the idea and getting some initial encouragement from social media, Tom met with a director he had worked with before, Dean Matthew Ronalds. After getting Dean interested, he is quickly connected to an investor through a colleague, Michelle Alexandria. The investor was looking for a mid-level film project to get involved in. The investor and the film both had the same budget range: $150–200K so a match was possible pending final approvals.

That was October and the American Film Market was right around the corner. Tom and the investors decided to meet at the Loews Hotel in Santa Monica to discuss the project during AFM. Just like that, *#Screamers* had gone from idea to fully funded film in only a few months! Though it might appear as a happenstance connection brought the film and the funding together by luck – the seeds were properly placed to sprout. First, the film was a marketable idea with a track record of financial success, i.e. found footage, horror film. Second, the budget was low, yet realistic. Third, the director and producer were a team that had delivered in the past, on budget. It was a strong investment and it wasn't a shock that they had little trouble securing an equity investor.

At this point in the process, there was still no script, just an outline. That's the case more often than you might think. Funding often comes together before the script. But the concept also demanded no script. Befitting the found-footage genre, the dialogue would be improvised. The concept of the film made the script secondary, even counterproductive. The production value would match the found footage genre. Scenes that demanded a lot of post-production polish in other films, would be better left unpolished in this genre.

Production

Line producer, Jason Torres, budgeted the film at $150K filming on location in Rochester, NY. New York is a 35% tax credit state and the 35% was split between returning some to the investor and investing some additional funds into the production. Rochester, NY is a non-permit, non-union county allowing the production to use SAG actors but not having to worry about union crew costs.

Post-production, early screenings and festivals

Tom notes a few lessons learned from the project. First, the production team was too enthusiastic. They screened the film for buyers too early. He thought the film was too long when it was screened by its prime prospective buyers. Test screen your film first to low-risk audiences who will give good, honest feedback but are *not* your top sales prospects. Twenty minutes was cut from the film but not before being passed on by some top buyers early in the process. When buyers pass on your film, normally, they will not take a second look at it even if you have substantially recut the film.

Second, Tom discovered that festival runs have a downside. Festivals date your film prematurely. *#Screamers* debuted, with some success, at festivals in 2016 and was dated a 2016 film permanently. Had they postponed their festival run, the film could have debuted in 2017. The year posted on IMDB carries a lot of weight with buyers and the film loses value if it's dated a prior year. A 2017 date would have let the sales team sell the film as "new" for an additional year.

Sales and final success

In the end, after editing the film, it was sold in most top tier territories. It sold to distributors in Germany, Brazil, the UK, France and others. Domestically, Dread – a specialist in horror films – bought the film. As is typical, roughly 75% of revenues came from foreign and 25% came from domestic sales. The film doubled its budget in terms of revenues. Even though it may have been overdone, found footage horror delivered (again) for the investor.

Movie: *Ashley* (2013)

Ashley is a fantastic example of a small movie, a first-time writer and a financial success. Tom had been working as a filmmaking mentor to a talented young writer named Domenic Migliore. Domenic's script about a young girl coming to terms with her sexuality struck Tom as perfect for the budding LGBT niche.

Tom's production company estimated the film could be completed for a tiny budget of $75K. Trick Candle Productions would invest 40% while the writer invested 40% also. The final 20% was brought in through outside investment.

The casting of the film was key. Nicole Arianna Fox (a recent winner of *America's Top Model*) had a big social media following. She auditioned and played the lead role without blowing the budget. Tom cast the second lead, Jennifer Taylor, by calling talent managers and explaining what sort of actress he needed. She was a recognizable face from a popular TV show (*Two and a Half Men*), so she was both an experienced actress and brought some value. Finally, by working their personal network through Tom's producing partner on the film, Brian Ronalds, the producers were able to bring Michael Madsen to set for a single day. The production utilized Madsen to the fullest and the film ended up with Madsen onscreen for ten minutes.

With just a small budget like this efficient production is also quite important. Shooting was kept to 13 days which mostly happened in Los Angeles at DC Stages – i.e. pre-built set stages that you can rent daily. Even though they had not presold the film at the markets, Tom did have a buyer in mind during production. From experience, he knew the best way to introduce a potential buyer to the film was *during filming*. If you can bring a potential buyer to the set, their enthusiasm for the project will be at a high point. Tom brought a potential buyer to the set the day that Michael Madsen was filming – the best possible day. The buyer, New Films International, wanted to own the film outright and offered twice the budget – $150K. Tom sold the film immediately for a 100% profit on the film's investment.

Since then Tom has hired Jennifer in two additional movies. Nicole Fox has since been in eight more movies. Meaning the film was both a financial success and advanced the careers of all involved.

Case study

Low-risk, low-budget sci fi – Jeffrey Giles

Jeffrey Giles of Automatic Entertainment GL, LLC sells, distributes and produces feature length motion pictures. Each year, he's been a reliable presence at American Film Market, Cannes, Berlin and all major film markets. Automatic does international and domestic sales but also produces their own pictures. They occasionally initiate a project's funding and production where they see an opportunity. Automatic finds certain genres more appealing from a financial standpoint. In particular, I talked with Automatic's manager, Jeffrey Giles, about their self-produced sci-fi films.

Automatic's process is an excellent study in how to make movies, while doing everything possible to limit the risk of equity investment loss. They typically do not initiate film funding until they know they can produce the film for less than the expected sales value. Jeffrey and Automatic will green light the picture when they know they have distributors lined up to buy it.

Start with distribution

> Begin with an end in mind.
>> (*7 Habits of Highly Effective People*, Stephen Covey)

Jeffrey stresses that all projects should start with a firm grasp on where they will end up: "Start with distribution," he says. Who's going to distribute the film? Where will it be seen? This likely isn't theaters since such a low percentage of films go to theaters. So, who will buy it? How much will they buy it for? Have these films been successful investments for these buyers in the past and, thus, will they continue to buy them into the future when a new one is available?

Whatever film is being considered, first there is legwork to find out which distributors have purchased films similar to this before. Mostly, their film profile does *not* include big-name cast – so they draw interest in other ways.

Audience familiarity

Jeffrey points out that audience familiarity is important. Buyers undoubtedly look for this in a film. Audience familiarity is a concept similar to drafting which we have already reviewed in the book. There has to be something about the film that the audience connects with prior to seeing it. Big-name cast, Jeffrey points out, is just a way to short-circuit audience familiarity. It gives people immediately something they know about the film, a familiar face and therefore they know something of what to expect. But casting big-name actors can be a very expensive way of buying audience familiarity. Automatic typically prefers to use other means.

Films like *Jurassic Expedition, Avengers of Justice, Robin Hood – The Rebellion* – look immediately familiar to viewers. These films by name association may also are similar to films that buyers have purchased before or have seen in the marketplace. Those buyers have had positive experiences with these films and therefore they have a strong appetite for buying movies with similar titles or marketing elements now.

Pitching buyers

The cast, the budget range, the genre – every aspect of the film is considered when sitting down with distributors. Have they bought films like this, with this production value, with this budget and type of cast before? Would they be interested in this film once it's done, assuming it is of similar quality to ones they have bought in the past? What sort of prices are they paying for these types of films? What sort of sales estimates would they give for these films? No film is given the green light until its pitched numerous times.

This means talking *directly* to foreign and domestic buyers before any film is funded. How is it pitched?

The package

The film package may contain: the title, premise, concept artwork/poster. The package also includes a director and a tentative cast. At this point, there may not be a script. The project package is shown to buyers all over the world at various markets. In the ideal scenario, buyers love the idea so much they put down money for a negative-pickup. In prior years, you could generate 50% or more of your budget from presales, now it's more like 0–30%.

However, even without a large percentage of the budget covered by pre-buys, Automatic can get confidence in the project by the interest levels of the buyers. If the film package gets enough pre-buys and/or enough interest, Automatic makes the first equity investment and takes the film package to investors.

Funding

The films that Automatic produces are funded by a combination of equity sources. Automatic plays the role of executive producer. A typical budget for these sci-fi films is within the SAG ultra-low or modified-low scale. Let's assume only 10% of a total $250K budget, $25K, has been raised in presales. As the rest of the funds are raised, Automatic is continuing to pre-sell the rights to territories, closing the gap on how much risk-oriented equity investment is required. Through this process of pitching the film to distributors for presales and pitching the film to investors for equity, it typically takes three to six months to raise the full budget.

As the film progresses through production, more assets are accumulated: photography, clips, talent associated, etc. This makes the sale more appealing and draws in more buyers. Presales will increase after principal photography is finished. With the film in post-production, presales speed up. It's not uncommon for 80% of the budget to be recouped by the time the film is finished!

Typical film timelines and other statistics

Their typical film is developed for roughly six months through pre-selling before the film's funding is raised. Another 12 months from funding to finished film makes a total of 18 months from concept to finished film. Films are being shot in 15–25 days, with as many as 800 post-production computer generated effects.

Advice to filmmakers

Many times, Automatic is following this exact same process in partnership with outside filmmakers who are bringing ideas to them. If a filmmaker brings a script, a relationship to a key actor, or some other kind of *value*, they can propose an idea to Automatic. If this is the type of project that Automatic feels will attract the interests of their buyers, they will often take an interest, source equity or perhaps invest. We have talked before about "bring it to someone that can do something with it." Automatic and companies like them are great examples of where you can take your ideas. They partner with new filmmakers regularly to develop, produce and pre-sell films to the markets. Having a good project to pitch companies like Automatic is a way to jump-start any filmmaking career.

Case study

Making 70 films with Daniel Zirilli of PopArt Film Factory

Daniel Zirilli has made over 70 films to date. He loves the action genre but also dabbles in wholesome family entertainment. Zirilli started his career by making a music video for his own band. His love for music was clearly matched by his talent for directing so once he began making music videos, he didn't stop there. He founded his company, PopArt Film Factory, at age 24 and has been prolific ever since.

After 70 films certain things get easier, but we tried to talk about what to do when you're starting out and lessons that can be applied when you don't have the long, successful track record. He and I discussed universal principals of making commercially viable films.

First, like many people in this business, he stresses: "All movies are risky, some less than others. There is no such thing as a safe movie investment. All you can do is stack the cards in your favor and work your ass off to make something creative and commercial – but there will always be risk in any investment."

Genre and structure

Zirilli's favorite genre is action with a close second being family entertainment. Most of our conversation revolves around his action work. "Action and thriller are great genres because a fight or chase scene is a universal, primal thrill. It works in any language."

We talked a bit about another genre that gets a lot of attention from low-budget filmmakers that want a reliable investment. "Horror has been overdone the last 20 years," he says. "It's like comedy," Zirilli says, "the issues internationally with comedy is that you don't know you have a really funny film until the film is done and you watch it in front of an audience. A similar thing is going on with horror where you don't know if it's really scary until you're done. Plus horror is a flooded market!"

Talking about action: "Usually, we have eight to ten action sequences, with careful structure and pacing. The opening needs to be strong," he says. Zirilli can hear the next question in his mind before I can even say it. We are both familiar with the objections of less experienced filmmakers. "Filmmakers need to understand that if they stick to a structure, it doesn't make them a sell-out. The structure is that way for a reason – because it works and can be exciting."

We talked quite a bit about an inexperienced filmmaker being worried about being a "sell-out." I mentioned my own challenges getting this project off the ground- including the time a film seminar instructor asked me why I wanted to make films that made money at all. The instructor's comment was "Why don't you want to make something good instead?" Zirilli's answer to that instructor: "That may be why that guy is giving seminars instead of making movies. Because of attitudes like that, unless you want to blow through someone else's money, and never make another film, it's better to make a movie that is artistically and commercially successful. Not just burn through money to show off to your supposed friends." Zirilli says.

Elevated thrills

Roger Corman insisted that his films be more than mindless entertainment. Roger gave each film a personal message – a "subtext," he called it. Something that Roger wanted to say about the world. Zirilli feels the same way about his entertaining action films. He strives for "elevated" action movies that make the audience feel for the characters. He prefers to show the human drama and the character studies at the center of the plot's conflicts. "There has to be a balance between the thrills in the film and the character drama. My favorite two action films are *Heat* and *Man on Fire*. Those films had great action but they are also awesome character driven dramatic films. The scene (in *Heat*) where DeNiro and Pacino meet in a coffee shop was the simplest scene in the world to film but there was so much at stake in the scene. It was fantastic."

Breaking down his process

Zirilli starts with a genre and a film he knows his distribution partners will buy. In a typical scenario, he's going to a distribution partner with the synopsis, treatment and proposed cast. He's not sending the script yet but has it ready in case they request it. You need sign-off and investment in the general concept and the film's treatment. Similar to many of our pro's, he's not thinking festivals as the landing place for his films, he's thinking distribution. "My current film, *Hollow Point*, is winning some awards at festivals but normally speaking, I don't spend a lot of time or energy with festivals. Doing a few key festivals can be good for reviews and exposure, but the goal should be getting a good worldwide distribution deal, not spending money and years on the road patting yourself on the back"

He takes the synopsis to sales and distribution companies with usually three proposed cast. First, the lead, that will carry the weight of the narrative and be on set the most. This probably isn't the biggest star. Second, one big-name star that will be on set fewer days. And third, a fun cameo from another star to round out the cast. These three cast usually make a good balance for the film to make it marketable around the world. With this, and Zirilli as a director, he is normally able to fund the entire film with presales. A typical scenario is $500K presold domestic and $500K in presold foreign. And often, he will film in a location that has a (plus or minus) 25% tax incentive/rebate.

Even though he has minimum guarantee contracts for amounts equal to the budget of the film, he still has equity investors because it's more advantageous to secure the presales contracts with private equity rather than a bank loan. "We could take these contracts to a bank and get a loan against them but now it's more efficient financially for us to go to a private equity firm. They advance us the funds to make the film. We often have 100% of the budget before we start. Sometimes we have more than 100% of the budget if we get tax credits where we are filming."

Advice to filmmakers

As good as that may sound for a filmmaker, Zirilli and I both know that it's not as easy for first-time or second-time filmmakers to presell their films for $1M and to get three name cast members. So, what about if you're starting out?

"The most important advice is to go develop unique material. It doesn't have to be a full script. It can be just a 1 page synopsis or treatment. I still take unsolicited material. If someone looks my info up, you can send me a 1 page synopsis. A lot of people don't take unsolicited material but some people still do. I delete full scripts sent to me but a short synopsis, I'll read."

You can submit a synopsis via Instagram to @DanielZirilli.

This is akin to the advice: bring something of value to the table, something unique. Another bit of advice goes out to the fellow directors out there: go shoot something. This is a smart twist on the "just do it" advice that many creative types give at SXSW and other festivals.

Instead of going and shooting a cheap film and praying: go shoot something short as an idea of what the film might look like. In fact, he did exactly that himself to get the funding for his feature *Time Rush*.

"For *Time Rush*, I went out and just shot 50 minutes for $30K. I made the most of that $30K. We rigged a car to *flip*, as well as extended hand-to-hand fights sequences. The first sales company I showed the teaser trailer to gave us the money to complete the film and a post deal. It was less than $100K to finish the movie. Because now cameras and technology are much cheaper, so work on your talent and directing chops, even on an iPhone, in 4k, and go out and make something that stands out, not just talking heads." You might not have $30K to shoot 50 minutes but even if you shoot 15 minutes, you are well ahead of most filmmakers asking for investment.

Fully developed scripts shouldn't be longer than 85–90 pages. Especially if it's action since action on the page takes more time than dialogue. Typically, a 90-page script will be a 90-minute movie but 90 pages that are action-heavy will be longer movies. Ninety pages that are dialogue-heavy will be a shorter movie. Therefore, a 110-page action script will be too long for an indie movie, will cost more, take more time to shoot, so best to keep it tight. Once you have a great commercially viable film idea: create a pitch deck, synopsis and logline. Pitch it to sales, distributors and financiers. But the key is to have something to show them that's unique and dynamic. Show footage and have a reel.

"I got my start shooting a music video for my own band because I wanted to get signed as a musician. The record company that I showed it to said: 'We're not gonna sign your band. but who shot your music video?' and boom I started shooting music videos."

His best advice is do what George Clooney did: "Develop unique material for yourself. Give yourself all the best parts ... then get that idea to someone that can do something with it."

This means partnering with business people in the industry. Partner with a producer, director, production company, distribution firm or sales agent that can take the idea and get cast or money for the project. Expand your rolodex beyond your immediate network of creatives and friends on set. If you bring something unique to someone that has been successful making these kinds of movies before, you are positioning yourself for success.

His other advice is about building relationships: "Do the right thing by people. Develop long term relationships in the business. And that means doing things for people and returning favors when people do things for you. Don't burn people. And that includes do everything you can to not lose people's money."

And with that, the advice comes back to where we began. The goal shouldn't be to find that one high-wealth individual that will invest in your film. Building your resume on top of someone else's loss isn't a great start to a career, nor good karma. The goal should be to do right by people and that means your investors too. The smart money in show business is getting too smart to invest in losing proposals. Having a strong film that will sell around the world is the best way to minimize risk. And that makes it more likely to get investment in the first place. So, go shoot something, but do everything you can to not lose people's money.

Index

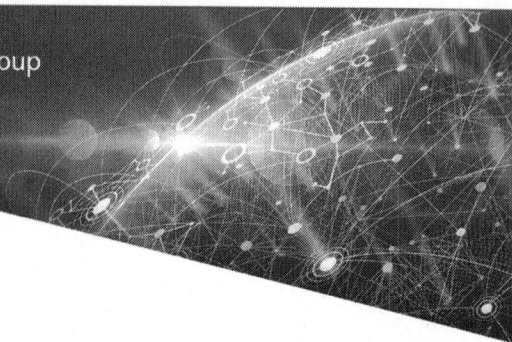